18 March 1989 2.30pm

*"Stop! Take up your pen and write..My words – to give,
to share, as a book to be called 'Diary of the Lord'..."*

8 February 2007 2.35pm

*"This book will water the hearts of people whose lives
have dried them out. Where oppression, stress, dilemma,
devastation, neglect or silence have desolated their
spirits, new life will sprout.*

Seeds sown long ago – of kindness, truth, gentleness,
power, strength, love and LIFE – will germinate, seeking
the Sun of God.*

His light alone will nourish and nurture.

*Readers of this book will find the Truth – and the Truth
will set them free."*

(* by God before birth)

"Deeply moving. You've just got to stop everything and write the book."
Phyl, 58; atheist.

"Thank you for *'Love- the River -Ocean of Timeless Love'*. I am feeling much better now. I think of the vastness of the ocean..that much Love. I keep those words in my Bible. And *'I Am the Bringer of Hope'* is so beautiful, especially the part of being held in His hand. It is like a personal love letter from Him to me. I want to savour it. I will take time and meditate on it. God is so good." Dorothy, 68, Roman Catholic.

"I showed some of these precious words from the *'DIARY'* to a Hindu friend and she asked if she could take some to her family in India."
Pauline, 48, Swansea, Community Church.
"I keep coming back to one piece in particular - *'I Was There in the Summer'*. It keeps making me cry. It was written just for me. Just for me!"
Ben, 22; no religious knowledge, interest, or experience .

"I copied *'I Am the Bringer of Hope'* and gave it to two other people. One of them was a man, full of anger from his time in the armed forces. I saw him the next day and his face had changed. He had read it and said he'd slept for the first time in ages and he had some peace. He couldn't remember when he last felt any peace. It's incredible!"
Monique,44, Christian.

"Because of these words, I have had the best time of my life with God. I am still crying since I read them yesterday. Please come to my country, the people need to hear these words. Just speak them – I will be your interpreter."
Simi, 23; Pentecostal church, Romania.

"I can't tell you what happened, or how grateful I am that you gave me again *'I Am the Bringer of Hope'*. It really spoke to me in a new way. By the time I had finished reading it, something actually changed – I was lifted into another place. I slept for the first time and I keep it under my pillow. I couldn't even read the Bible, but this brought me back and I can pray again now...I believe *'DIARY of the LORD'* will be a major resource for people to dip into. At times of need they will find something comforting that speaks exactly into their situation." M, 45, suffering divorce.

DIARY
of
THE LORD

BethBaraBooks

DIARY of THE LORD

First published in Great Britain in 2008
by BethBara Books

A CIP Catalogue of this book is available from the British Library

ISBN 978-0-9560961-0-4

Bethbara Books
PO Box 353
Denmead
Waterlooville
PO7 8FB
Tel. 07707044353
e-mail: info@bethbarabooks.co.uk

Printed and bound in Great Britain by the MPG Books Group
- with the writer's appreciation.

*For any one who wants to know if
God is real*

Thanks

To the many people, known and unknown to me, who have read or heard pieces of the *'DIARY'* and wanted more;

to Anita and Margareta, whose first reading of the messages to date in 2003 encouraged me to set out on the path ahead – and to Anita, again, for unfailing wisdom and faithful, prayerful support;

to friends in deed Peter and Helen, Margareta, Anita, Kerry and Doreen, for financial blessing to production; to Shirley and Maureen, precious prayer partners and 'book ends';

to dear Charlynne, for kindly and sensitively reviewing the manuscript, asking pertinent questions and consistently encouraging the route to publishing; to the Reverend Richard Thomas, inspiring leader of a celebratory family pilgrimage to Israel in 2006, whose luminous humility, integrity and scholarship promised a sound reading - and who responded to the Lord's prompting by giving a written response, now the Foreword;

to my son Adam, for his life-giving humour and radical example of fiery faith; to my son Lindsay, whose loving and listening heart embraces the world and generates joy and hope; and to my generous husband Pete, the 'rock' of love and blessing in my life – and whose talent captured the beauty of creation that covers the *'DIARY'* :
 my heartfelt gratitude and love.

And **to the Lord**, whose book this is, **ALL** honour and praise.

Contents

Foreword
Preface
DIARY of the LORD

11

Foreword

This is a remarkable book. It is a collection of messages or letters from the Lord to His children on earth.

They embrace a number of concerns that God has for his world: his love for everyone of his children; his demand for purity in their lives; his longing to remove burdens from their shoulders; his desire to renew and make whole their lives; his hope that those who love Him will love others around them; and many more.

The language throughout is very Biblical, though there are very few direct quotations from Scripture. Often one can imagine one is listening to one of the Old Testament prophets – Hosea or Micah, Isaiah or Jeremiah – the language is very similar and many of the themes could be what God was saying to His people Israel.

Here are a few very brief summaries of some of the messages.

"Accept My love for you and go out and love the world."

"Let My river of love sweep your burdens away."

"Brokenness is the key to receiving My love and happiness is the result as I lead you forward."

"My love is to be shared and poured out as a blessing to all mankind. I am coming to spend time with you. Be prayerful and let My Spirit water you through prayer and the Word. Make time for contemplation."

"Purify yourselves, be made whole. My tears will purify the souls of the departed. Be anointed and made holy."

"Blessed are those who call on My Name. Be still in My

presence and sacrifice yourself to Me. Seek Me and know My love for you."

"Do not fear. The place of fearlessness is the place of abiding. Go out with Me to tell people of God's truth."

"Come to the Feast of Tabernacles for bread and to give your bread. Nourish yourself or you will die."

Many will find this book a great blessing – drawing them closer to God, experiencing His love for them at a very deep level, leading them to a fuller repentance from sin, greater purity of life and urging them to go out and love others and tell them of God's love.
It could be divided into short devotional books, which I believe many people would find extremely helpful.

The Reverend Richard Thomas.

Preface

Nothing about God is discrete or can be boxed and all life streams from Him. So, I suppose I shouldn't be surprised by difficulties in trying to package His book; or by struggling over background information which, at best, could only be a snapshot, and may be of no real help. Should I even try to explain? To deal with the issues, I have tried imagining the *'DIARY of THE LORD'* from a new reader's perspective – but having lived with the flow of these words since 1986, it is a task too far from me. Therefore, what can I offer, apart from what I know?

The messages are offered to *"all the children of Israel"*, all people everywhere, in an arms wide-open embrace that stretches beyond the cultural and religious mindsets of organised churches. The embrace seems to rely on only two connected questions for the reader: Do you know God? Do you want to?

The words themselves stir our spiritual depths and God alone can answer the questions that may arise from that stirring. As the original questioning reader, I can say I have discovered that He is *always* ready and waiting with love. Sometimes, He answers with a new level of understanding. Sometimes, His apparent silence can leave us in tears and we can freely choose to wait longer or leave His way. I have found that staying with Him is worth the wait, *every* time.

He, alone, can touch our core...the place where He finds us uniquely precious, because we are made in His image. Where we disagree with His lovely view of us, He gently repairs and heals our perceptions of ourselves until we can agree. He teaches us to love ourselves properly and gives us the essential love and grace to value others. He removes the world's clouded lens and offers us His clearer one...if we want it.

These messages are a transparent display of His astonishing love – gentle, descriptive, encouraging, exhorting, correcting, challenging, appealing and inviting. They cross boundaries of belief and unbelief, speaking to the hearts of people who might want to know Him.
The words carry healing. For me, finding an early message slipped in to an old book was a lifeline at a desperate time in my life when I was too angry with God to pray or touch Scripture. Like a tiny candle in a long tunnel, it pierced the darkness surrounding me. Perhaps I should explain a little...
Beginning in 1983, God used several different people in various places to give me His instruction: *"Learn to listen."* No-one who expressed the instruction could explain it to me and for three years I was frustrated. Then, at 3 am one April morning in 1986, while my family were peacefully sleeping, God suddenly woke me up and began to let me hear Him dictating.
'DIARY of THE LORD' is His desired result of what He wanted to say over the following twenty years. He alone chose the times and opportunities to speak, breaking in through a backdrop of precious family life that has also been impacted by birth, lots of death, sickness, loss, breakdown, student life, broken careers, murder, trauma, and five house moves, some to and fro across the country. He has also given unspeakable joy, miraculous physical healing of my sons and myself, and grace beyond measure to overcome everything entirely in His strength. I have no independent resources or strength left – and I have never felt better equipped or safer in my life.
I have been too busy with everyday demands to ever occupy an ivory tower (much as I might have liked the chance at

times!); and I have not lived anywhere long enough to root or fit fully into any particular church congregation, so I cannot offer any ministry credentials to readers who might want them. I am just the amanuensis He called me to be, with a testimony of endless healing and grace to tell at another time.

I was never expecting a message and most came at random times when I was not prepared. Consequently, they were scribbled on scraps of paper or backs of envelopes, or whatever I could find in a hurry when I was interrupted while, perhaps, cleaning the bath. Not until the end of 2002, when I started to therapeutically type the messages, did I have any sense of what He had given me; and it was then He revealed that the book He had named and instructed me to write in 1989 – and for which I was still waiting – was already taking shape.

I take most seriously the instruction in Jeremiah 23 v.28 *"..but let the one who has my word speak it faithfully"*; therefore, each piece is first draft, including form, punctuation and emphasis, determined as and when He gave it. Apart from removing some small distinctly private lines, the pieces in this collection are unaltered and for sharing. Where any link with me is evident, it is because there is apparent purpose for others in showing it. Perhaps another reader will be going through a hard place and gain enough encouragement from noticing the gentle way that the Lord heals and admonishes to trust Him with a little more of their life. In places where the Lord speaks graciously and intimately, it is to show His lovely tenderness so that someone might then want to seek Him for themselves.

The extended **Footnotes** include some hopefully appropriate background reference; and, where personal insight or opinion can be detected, it is neither prescriptive nor definitive and is more a glimpse of my hotchpotch soul. I just

17

hope that any irritant can become a pearl for a spitting reader. The main purpose of the Footnotes is to offer the initial and partial understanding that came with the messages, without the addition of research, validation or reflection. Therefore, they are subjective and without authority; and, while my aim is to help, a discerning reader may not feel the need to consider them.

The exception to this could be the footnote to the extraordinary last piece *"Today's Bread - Come to the Feast of Tabernacles"* **24 February 2006**, which brings together the old and new memorials, as a metaphor for the future of the whole church. At the time of receiving it I knew nothing about the Jewish feast, but I have briefly included my findings for the ease of any similarly uninformed reader.

Each reader's deepening personal understanding of anything in the *'DIARY'* will necessarily depend on God's preferred direction; and a dictionary, Bible and Concordance are invaluable guides to an open heart.

Although there are contextual stories behind some of the pieces, only two are included: one with *'Hope'* **29 January 1988** and the other accompanying *'Love Call'* **21 February 1989**; and these are separated into a short **Journal** extract at the end of the 80s section. These factual accounts demonstrate God's wonderful concern for people and His determined intention to heal them.

His love flows through the messages, calling us to spend time with Him, to know Him so that His Word can nourish us. He urges us to consume life-giving Scripture and to be consumed by it - and to pour ourselves and our cares into Him, so that He can turn us, too, into lovers.

The proof of the *'DIARYOF THE LORD'* is in the reading. The voice of the Author is clear. People have been deeply touched both by reading and hearing the messages. Regardless of age or culture, they impact those without faith and those who

18

want more, bringing to each something deeply personal.

Ben is someone who has had no experience or knowledge of God in his twenty-two years. He said: "I keep reading one piece. It makes me cry. It was written just for me – JUST for ME."

The piece that touched Ben so deeply was *"I Was There in the Summer" August* **1997**. Why would someone repeatedly return to something that kept moving him to tears, unless those tears were healing tears? In a profound way beyond his understanding, that he somehow recognised and then wanted, Ben's tears were a rite of passage to a better interior place. Only God can do that. Maybe one day, Ben will realise that, too.

Or, as Simi, a totally committed 23 year-old Romanian Pentecostal, said: "Because of these words - *"I Am the Bringer of Hope"* **11 December 1991** - I have had the best time of my life with God!"

The Father explained it like this :

"Wounds are deep and raw in My world and I long to pour balm, blood, into them. The blood is My Son's and the balm is the oil of gladness.

Tomorrow is a day that never comes for My dying. They look with deadening eyes for a sign of hope. They long for a life free of pain and suffering and only I have the answer for them.

The words you write will be part of their long-awaited answer. MY words will bring release, bring wholeness to hearts devoid of life."

(from *"Your work...Help Build My Sanctuary"* 11.20 am 28 June 2005)

DIARY of the LORD

CONTENTS 1986 - 89

5th April 1986 3 am

"JOIN IN THE FEAST OF SALVATION
..DAY OF THE LORD"

"Take into your mouths the words of My heart and eat, that you may be satisfied and grow in My ways. 1
For I place before you a table of feasts, designed with your needs in mind, upon which I place the fruits of My labours - My promises.

Take upon your selves My burden, My yoke of peace, for such would I ask of the world that I might bless the world. It is not easy. It will not come to pass until the rebellion of My people is vanquished. Be a stone upon the altar of My sacrifice, for love of My Son, for love of My people.

Join in the feast of salvation 2 and sit at the table of righteousness that a land may be delivered of her sons and daughters; whereupon My Spirit will descend upon the earth in a mighty torrent.

Go forth and spread My word. Tell it to your neighbours, tell it to your friends. Take the courage in your hearts that I would give you to do My bidding. Do not be afraid for My word will be accomplished according to My will. For I am supreme.

Do not fear injustice, although you will suffer it. Alone you may stand, surrounded by wolves, but such is My protection that no harm will come to you. This is My promise. Hold fast to My

23

words that the day of the Lord may be prepared.

Look towards your own and never doubt My promises. For I have given you a gift of priceless worth, exceeding even the stars - My love.

This is a gift to be shared and not to be kept to yourselves. Discover the delight of My heart and grow pleased in My sight at My provision - for this delights Me, too. Grow in a world where my voice is unleashed and unknown and take the gift that I give you to the starving millions who have never heard Me.

My time is short to make these pleas. So heed My voice, for the sake of your brothers and sisters.

Worry not about how to speak - I will give you the words.
Be willing tools in My hands that I may fashion for Myself a Kingdom of believers that the end may be averted which would bring destruction of My beautiful world. For the beauty that it holds is still there, untarnished but hidden from the eyes of unbelievers. The hope with which I would fill their hearts is not a gift for the blind - so open the eyes of My people, with a word from My voice. My word will accomplish its purpose when it leaves the mouth of a willing servant.

Trust in Me and see the day of My coming for I am at hand.
Settle the believers with a smile and bring to Me the unaccounted, drawn into your outstretched arms by the love you show them.

For this is My message to you that you love the world, whatever the cost, and be not mindful of it. Only pay the price of My flowing love and you will discover no cost at all. You will be released into a new place of being, where My love can flow and where you can live redemptively.

Claim the freedom I am offering that you may pass through the restrictions of self doubt and fulfil the humanity I first dreamed of. Take My love, My people, as I offer up a sigh for your release. **For I have finished dreaming and I have started planning the day of My return.**

It is My wish to see My dreams fulfilled.

A time of justice, a time of peace, is not beyond the imaginings of man, but within his grasp if he turns to Me.

Such is the division that you may feel you stand alone, but this will never be true. Uphold My word, trust in My Son and you will always be comforted. For this is the day of the Lord. Proclaim it with boldness and with joy."

Sunday 27 July 1986   9.10 am

"LOVE - THE RIVER... OCEAN OF TIMELESS LOVE"

"For behold I gave you a Son - a Son whose glory will shine before nations, whose words shine like molten silver.
More precious than the gift of life is the gift of My Son. Into His arms I placed the world, that it may be encompassed by love - a love so divine that nothing can stand against its strength.

Lay hold on the key to this Love. Draw into a well whose depths are timeless and which can heal the past. Wash in a love that purifies. Bathe in the love that refreshes. For in it you will be made whole and the future will hold no uncertainties - for the depths are timeless.

Bring all your burdens ₁ to this pool of love and see how easily they float from you - only themselves to rest on the surface of My love. Let them bob away like corks in the ocean, for that is all they are. If you leave them in love, will Love not carry them safely? Was it not your love, an imperfect love, which caused you to carry them in the first place? How much more certain can you be, then, that the endless ocean of perfect love will carry them better?

Consider yourself as a carrier loaded with the hurts of others, whose job is to bring these hurts to be healed, rather as freshly mined jewels need to be washed. How then can you claim these hurts as your own?

27

You come to the rolling ocean of love and enter the waters. Your burdens are washed from you and you are revitalised, to continue on your journey. But you collect more and need to return to wash sooner.

Each time you emerge from the purifying waters, you are yourselves greater in love - and you seem to be unable to journey any distance before being burdened. And this is My Plan - that <u>you live in the flow of Love</u>, so strengthened that others are drawn wholly to you, that you may set them free of the burdens that they carry. You will be living springs wherein others bathe away the hurts and concerns they carry for themselves and even others. 2 And the process will repeat and thus My love will wash the world.

All roads on this journey lead to love. You yourselves are at the water's edge.

Place into My care the troubles that hinder you from stepping into the refreshing waters. Or come in fully laden and bathe in a love so gentle, so uplifting, that a heart would yearn for a mere drop of the living water.

And I offer you an <u>ocean</u> – an OCEAN of TIMELESS LOVE; which, even as you bathe, reaches into the past and heals hurts tenderly; which brings to the future a gentle certainty, as that future becomes now. I release you to live <u>now</u>.

Love is the moment lived fully, creatively, beautifully, purposefully in My blessing, in My Presence. I offer you a lifetime of these moments and I stand at the door, laden with blessings and riches.

Will you, <u>this</u> moment, invite Me in to distribute My gifts of Love? Each to each and an abundance of variety.

I come to encourage, uplift, admonish, empower and release."

28

1st January 1987   3.15pm

"INTO THE MOUTHS OF CHILDREN"

"Get up! Get up! Rise up and shout praise to the Lord your God. For in Him all creation lives. And the newness of all life shall be revealed in a heart of tenderness. For upon these lips I place a new song - a song of majesty and splendour, to reverberate and echo throughout the halls, throughout the land.

Into the mouths of children I will place Hosannas, so loud and sweet, to drown the efficiencies of the world. And a new awakening will burst forth and a river of joy will sweep this place, washing all before it. And it will come from the mouths of the babes." 1

2 January 1987 12.35pm

"FROM THE FOREHEAD OF YOUR SON"

"From the forehead of your son will come a star of light 1
which will dazzle onlookers. And in the East a star will rise,
this day, of the same name.
And this will be a sign unto you.

For in this day of our Lord, great things are happening.
Tumultuous movements are beginning which will reverberate
throughout the world: and the blackness is being shaken.
*For the angel has sounded the horn - the first angel, the first horn.*2
And the time has begun."

6th January 1987

"GENTLE, PURIFYING RAIN"

"My Spirit flows…Into hearts so dark, so burdened.
Gentle, purifying rain will fall, washing away sin and guilt
and bringing new life to blossom once again."

"MY WORDS SHALL NEVER DIE
..I SEEK ONLY THE LOVE OF MAN"

"Into your spirit I am pouring a newness, an equity of such magnitude that Heaven's doors will be flung open and riches will pour down.

A new life awaits you.

Around the sea of uncertainty I will place a band of restriction. No turbulence will endure the constraint of My heart and I WILL ENCOMPASS the problems WITHIN ME. Into My heart I will absorb the concerns and they will be forever safe and secure in My love.

Lives will prosper in My glory. My riches will be seen by many and will be a sign and witness of My love. For famine is over and plenty arrives on the wings of prayer.

Turn your face to the coming Lord and look full in His wonderful face, as He turns His gaze on you.

Be abundant in your love and share the promises with others. For what I do for you, I do for many.

And My words shall never die, or change, as My path is unalterable.

I seek only the love of man in return for the abundance of My kingdom and My words WILL find homes. As I whisper words of love in to the ears of the hungry, many hearts will turn and open to Me.

The gentleness of Spirit is great and is all you need to rest on. So rest, <u>learn to rest</u>, and in the stillness of your heart I will come to you, to accomplish My will in your life and, through you, in the lives of others.

Be at peace and know that I am the Lord who knows and loves you. For in this hour has come the time to surrender your heart to Me. For I WILL live in a pure heart and My Being has peace within you.

Be at peace and fear not for My time, and your time, is at hand.

Into your mind I will pour the words of longing, longing for My Spirit. Deep utterances will be made and rend your heart. Be at peace and know that My Spirit is accomplishing a work of honour and magnitude, in preparation for an infilling of light and glory.

Be at peace and know My name - I AM."

24th October 1987

"FOR MARY IS THE MOTHER OF MY CHILD"

"For Mary[1] is the mother of My child - a sceptre of peace [2] in an age of darkness. Her beauty shines forth today [3] even amid the torrents and deluge of abuse that fall from unsuspecting mouths. [4]

For many have not yet seen or acknowledged the presence and power of My mother. Her presence will beautify your life and the gates of Hell will not prevail against her.

Her presence is a thing of beauty, of love, and of great blessing - a token bestowed by Me upon the world, of My great love.

For to whom would I entrust My precious mother if not to those who would reverence and care for her?[5] Her presence in a world of bleakness is to <u>enhance</u> the power of God, NOT challenge it.

For she serves Me, even now. And her time is yet to come.

For there will be a great upsurge of devotion to her, brought about by the prayers of the faithful; and through her, many more thousands will come to Me.[6] For she is a way of truth, of beauty, of justice within which captives [7] flourish.

When they cannot find the Way,[8] they can find a mother's arms and these arms I offer you. I would say again to you ...

"Step again into the comfort of the loving arms of My mother. You have nothing to fear and much to gain. Even then your own

33

mother will be restored to you. As a bridge, My mother will carry you to yours and place you again in the tender, loving arms of your own mother, a woman whose hurt is very deep and very real.

For she too was deprived. She was deprived of your love, as surely as you were deprived of hers. But she lost yours first. Separation is a cruel thing and I would heal your mother's loss by restoring you to her arms. ₉

I offer to you the arms of My mother to restore and reconcile you, as a baby to a mother, that the mother may be reconciled and restored to the baby. ₁₀

These are deep things I am speaking about and the fulfilment is a short time away. Take notice of these words and act upon the devotion I am giving you.

Take into your heart the instruction to revere My mother, that I may bring wondrous things to pass. For in this healing many miracles will be seen, evidenced to all; that the life of the family may be complete. And so your motherhood.

For in these days I am placing within you a seed of justice, that My word on this matter is spread far and wide. Overcome your prejudice, planted by men, that My word this day is complete.

*Trust not your heart - trust **Mine** - for would I show you anything but love? Would I reveal to you things unjust, unrighteous, unloving? Can I be other than I AM?*

Can you not see, can you not hear the words being poured out for you? Do you not realise the magnitude of the blessing that I am pouring upon you?

*I would have you know Me as **LORD.** I would have you know Me as son, as lover, ₁₁ as friend, as brother, as all in all to you.*

For I am calling you into a place of understanding, where darkness

34

looms but cannot overcome you. ......

...A devastation will fill the hearts of man and much suffering will ensue, but the love of a mother will survive even this, and for this reason I am restoring you this day to yours and to Mine.

    <u>My</u> mother's love will encircle and enfold you and <u>your</u> motherly love will encircle and enfold others. Your mother will be restored to you, wholly and completely, and the bitterness of past years melted away. For in her is a love which I have breathed, a flame so bright that it is inextinguishable, despite all severity and odds. Honour her and allow <u>My</u> mother to show you how.

    For <u>My</u> mother is tender, loving, dutiful, protective, forgiving, forbearing and enduring and knows how to <u>receive</u> love. Practise <u>giving</u> love, for you do not yet know how, to <u>My</u> mother, that <u>your</u> mother benefits from your growth.

    Let <u>My</u> mother show you how to be a dutiful daughter, able to honour and care in a loving and gentle way for the needs of the woman who bore you. Let <u>My</u> mother reveal this woman's needs that you see her more clearly as a person, and not just as an extension of yourself.

    Do not be afraid to ask <u>My</u> mother for help, as I give her to you now, to draw on, in understanding and in deepening knowledge and wisdom of what it is to mother and be mothered. Ask her how <u>she</u> responded to her own mother while growing up.

    Let her retrace your childhood with fingers of love, writing in your heart restored, healed and perfected responses. Be made whole and complete in the shadow of the greatest woman who ever lived that the womanliness I bestow on you is a testament and constant reminder of her presence in your life.....

.... And the love of your family, within your family, will withstand with fortitude slings and arrows of outsiders and will do much to *restore the status of family in the eyes of others.*

Guard against pride and self justification *- you have no need of either, for My Presence will justify you and your actions, and this will be seen by those who need to know. Suffer the misunderstandings of others without the eyes to see and be glad of a share in My suffering, for in it you will find even more of Me.*

*Do not be afraid to use your mind, to **think** in response to My Presence - for can I not answer **every** question? Can I not meet **every** challenge?*

Would I not welcome the opportunity to take you further into the mind of Christ?

Did I not equip you, before time began, for such a journey? Why else did I bless you with the little of your mind that you know? Release it now, to Me, and think with me that I, the Master, the Teacher, may lead you, My pupil, as you enter into My MIND.

For this is My parting gift to you this day - freedom from self-imposed restraint and entry into dialogue with Me which will astound you, as I reveal to you time-honoured truths and secrets reserved for My followers.

I will lead you into deserts where only My voice will be heard and the apprenticeship will be hard. But I am preparing you....

...But first yield to Me the first fruits of your heart, that I might better teach you the path of sacrifice.12

We have an exciting path to travel as I teach you. Spend many hours with me, that I might instruct and admonish you, to form for Myself your new character...

*Leave all things to Me, all worries and cares and concerns, that I might better prepare you to receive Me, your **living LORD**.*

For I love you and I always will."

9 January 1988   2.04 am

'HOPE'   1

"And there came upon the land a great blessing; and that blessing was called Hope; a blessing so great that Hell could not prevail against it.

People's eyes were opened to the glory of the King and ashes fell from their eyes. Everything that had blinded them fell away and a great vision was given to them.

In the days of the outpouring of My Spirit, Hope shall be an abundant blessing. For I can change all things. A glimpse of Hope will excite the nations and many will rise up in joy, proclaiming the name of Jesus. But an abundance of Hope will bring forth change in the spirit of My people and people will reach out to grasp the possibilities offered to them.

Light will flow in abundance and all that is, seen and unseen, will change according to My glory, says the Lord, and people will be hungry to grasp My truth.

So Hope flows on My anointed ones, like a mighty river, to wash away the curse of darkness that envelops and imprisons even My chosen ones.

Step into My stream of Hope and be made new.

All old understanding will be washed away with the constraints of the mind. The shackles of trained and cultured thoughts will disappear and the shining clarity of real vision will emerge, flowing

37

and unlimited, with no blind alleys of dead-end intellect to halt progress like a sealed maze.

A wind of change will blow through your minds and the breath of the Spirit will warm the untouched recesses of your mind, setting free blocked and imprisoned emotions and responses. What was frozen will melt in the warmth of His breath and life will flow again.

I come to set people free, says the Spirit, and to bring the joy of God to all believers. For the joy of God is **My** understanding, **My** way of looking at the world. Fear the darkness no longer, but bathe in the light of My coming; for a day will soon come when nations will stand before Me and cry "Abba, Father" and My glory will be known.

Enhance your lives with the presence of My Spirit, a welcome visitor who desires to stay. Make Him welcome and invite Him into your hearts and know the care-free love of God. For the Father will not mislead you, or let you down. He desires only your good; and gentle hearts abound in this place, a fitting place to lodge.

For I have found you worthy, says the Lord. I have counted you all among My blessings and no greater love than Mine shall ever be poured out upon you.

Step into this love and be made holy. Cast all your fears aside and just receive. Receive the love of the Father, the Spirit of the Son and the Son Himself, a three-fold unity to bind your body, soul and spirit together. Within this unity no harm shall befall you and I shall leave no loop-hole for the Devil to attack you.

I shall seal you this day in the perfection of My image and in all things you shall be made whole.

Many have wandered and lost their way, in search of better, brighter, sounder ideas. But ideas have confused them and dogged their lives. Philosophies will abide and theologies will dominate, but only in the world's eyes.

The truth which passes all understanding is a gift to set all men free from their ideas and their search for meaning. Ideology is not truth and truth is a gift for _you_ to share. It is only found in Me.

_I Am_ the _only_ Source. In Me is everything safe and well, easy and hard. For I will change _all_ things to good, for those who love Me.

Love is all you need. Love is the greatest gift My Spirit can bestow. Love flows before you and opens the door to many hearts.

For I would release you this day to a place of wandering the earth in search of My beloved, My lost children. To you it is given to bring them back to Me, to bring them home to the place of warmth and love that they once knew.

Ask, and the desires of your heart will come to pass, for you are a people dear to My Heart. I have called you by name, to suffer for My sake and to experience and witness to My glory.

Call My people back. Go and find the lost sheep, already searching for the fold. Draw those who once belonged to Me back to the truth of My presence within them. Search the by-ways for people tired of searching, defeated by struggle and strain, who settle for what they already know.

Let My Presence in you be known in the smile on your lips, in your eyes and in your heart.

The quietness of your look, your gaze, will convey Me to the wounded, so do not be afraid of what I Am asking you to do.

An anointing will be poured out upon you in the going along the *path. As you travel in My footsteps you can trust My presence within you to guide you. Do not look for <u>sign posts</u> to direct you, but lean heavily on My Spirit - and know and realise the presence of your Lord who loves and comforts you at all times.*

Do these things in memory of Me, the Good Shepherd, and My mantle will cover and protect you at all times. Have no fear, but move and speak only in My <u>love</u> and not in <u>your understanding</u>. For I will give you words, to repeat and to rejoice, and the Kingdom will come and have no end. For all time I Am making this promise to you - that the days of your life will be numbered by the stars in Heaven and that for all eternity you will know Me as your Lord.

Just say this to My people - that I, the Lord, have spoken."

(A background story to this piece is in the JOURNAL section.)

30 April 1988 8.25 am

"THE TREE OF LIFE......I AM THE MASTER BUILDER"

From the depth of despair a new tree will bloom - the tree of life. Life-enhancing love will blossom and bear fruit and this is My promise to you this day.

For often I have watched you, labouring in the vineyard of souls with no thought for yourself, and wondered how long it would be before I could love you to wholeness and completeness yourself.

This time has come.

From the depths of your very brokenness new seeds will flourish. The death that you know now will yield new life - within you and without you.

For the brokenness of your being is a sign to me of your readiness to receive Me. So far you have only been touched, so lightly, by Love. Now the time is coming, is near, when Love may consume you - restore you, revive you, resurrect you, flow through you, course through your veins as life-giving Blood - the Blood of sacrifice - and engulf you in its fire.

For the pain you feel will be terrible and the hurt enamoured of Me 1

My tidings for you are of joy - a bitter blossom at the moment, since you cannot yet see its production.

Many days will pass before the outpouring of this love and these will be days of testing, of refining.

> *For those I love, I prune. For those I love, I test in the Refiner's fire. For those I love, I burnish with the Firemaker's cloth - to gleam triumphant in this dark world.*

I am opening up for you a vista of humanity which will tear your heart and ache your being.

The troubled world we live in has many tortures to endure - self inflicted in most cases.

The Day of Judgement is at hand and I, the Lord, will endeavour to speak words of comfort to My people.

Be of cheer and enter My heart - encourage others to do the same.

It is the only safe refuge. Mary will help this passage to My heart. Trust her and her guidance and seek her help often, in all things - for I have given her to you, to reverence and obey. Her guidance is pure and simple, like a child's heart, and her endeavours will render the hearts of her followers similarly.

Be at peace and know that this undertaking is huge - but that you are equipped for this journey....to enter My heart.

I have called you by name for this journey and suffering humanity is the path you have to take.

*Do not seek to hurry this step - it will take time to establish its foundation. I am the **Master Builder**. My hand is firm and strong, My eye is true. I <u>never</u> make mistakes. My choice of materials is perfect; and I have chosen the best today for the best results tomorrow.*

*Be at peace and know that I am the **Helmsman** who guides and steers you through stormy waters. **Welcome the turbulence as a sign of MY presence.***

Remember that I am shaking loose all things not of Me that bind one to another. So do not be surprised at these changes in you. Rather, rejoice and see My hand shaping and improving.

Unless you come to Me, to seek Me from the depths of your need, I cannot reach you to minister to your needs, for your heart will not be open to receive Me.

My gift is a gift of longing for succour and comfort within My heart and you will yearn unceasingly for My presence and comfort.
Brokenness is the key.
Happiness is the fruit of this death. Abiding love is the sign for you, and the world, of My presence within you.

For what I have given, is given freely for all time; and I never take back My gifts.
Tend them well in the garden of your heart and let My Father, the Gardener, water and prune you, that the harvest from this Tree of Life will be abundant."

Tuesday 2 May 1988 11.10 pm

"Prayer and fasting every Friday for suffering humanity is the way into the

Lord's heart." (Mary) 2

43

19th October 1988   11.05 am

"THE COMING OF MY KINGDOM WILL BE
UPON THE LAND"

"The day of the Lord is fast approaching and the coming of My Kingdom will be upon the land. Insight will be granted to all who keep My Word and the faith of My followers will ensure survival of an age so dark that mountains shudder in disbelief and horror.

Fear and trembling will be upon the masses of captives whose minds and spirits have been chained by evil in its many and various manifestations.

Your mission is to set these captives free.

Again I say to you that the day of the Lord is fast approaching. Be ready, be on hand for the days of deliverance. Many will fall by the wayside in the tumult that follows the clarion call of the Lord.

Be among those who stand firm by bathing in My Word, whose presence 1 will uplift you and carry you high above the plagues of pestilence which shall cover the face of the earth.

My Word is eternal, is truth, is life-giving, encouraging to all who would listen.

Listen often to My voice as the blessings of the Lord shower upon you.

Before all time and between all ages man has stood firm in the Lord and the Body has been maintained.

A day is coming when the Body will be shattered and scattered bringing desolation to the hearts of many. Be among My

44

comforters. Bring healing to My wounded body. Let all men know that I, the Lord their God, will show mercy to the end of time. There is nothing I will not forgive, if people will only turn to Me. Only then will they see My face and know My will.

For in these tidings, great truth is contained. The message of an angel brought forth peace and joy and love; but the message of a good and faithful servant will bring forth change.2 Destruction and desolation will be restored to wholeness. Life will replace living death. Barrenness will give way to fertility of thought and word and deed - and My Kingdom shall have <u>no end.</u>

Seek Me, often, at all times, for all things and ventures which will be a means of bringing people to Me.
I am hungry for souls - eager to feed My lambs and sheep; for I have much to give.
None will go to waste as the abundance of My Presence is poured out upon My people.
Love is My gift to you and to all. A love which transcends barriers, crosses time, heals and is immortal.

My Spirit will fall upon mountains and cause them to collapse. My Spirit will fall upon dams and cause them to burst. All will be swept away before the might and power of the Lord.
But destruction <u>will</u> cease. Peace will be restored. Love will rule and govern the hearts of My people.

For I am calling to Myself the people of My pasture. I myself will shepherd them and no boundaries will hold or limit them.

45

Be ready for the Day of Judgement. Weep and lament for the forgotten ones whose families leave them in the throes of Hell. 3

On Earth a tumultuous outpouring of grief will cause abandonment in hearts but I will restore.

Be at hand to hear My voice and do My will. Know that I am causing great upheavals in the lives of many, for the time has come to be cut loose and set free from all not of Me that binds, one to another.

Only My love is sufficient; only My love is good enough to bind without chains; to release without loss; to restore and reconcile without interruption and to make whole and complete all the fruits of My love.

For I have anointed you; for I am anointing you; for I have called you by name to be holy. Cleave only unto Me and draw breath from Me. Breathe only in My Spirit; breath of My breath upon you and within you.

Utter <u>only</u> words of peace and understanding. Give all else to me. Give to Me all your thoughts, ideas, interests, inclinations, that I may fashion them for My pleasure and for My perfect plan.

Rest, and be certain that I the Lord am speaking to you, this day.

And this shall be a sign unto you. You shall go forth into the desert of souls and bring forth fruit for My pleasure."

21 February 1989

LOVE CALL

"Love is like a flowing stream that
Washes people free
From grime and stress and sin and fear
The more they come to Me.

To bathe within My waters,
To cleanse in waves of love,
Brings joy and peace and purity
- A gift from heaven above.

So do not fear to come, My child,
And enter deep within,
For there the love of God you'll find
- A life that's free from sin.

And nothing then will harm you
Your fears will come to nought,
For deep within My Spirit burns
Your life with blood He bought.

My life alone 1 is for you
As you step this way
Into My stream forever,
And love Me alone2 and pray.

47

Fear not to ask for guidance,
In all things know My name * 3
That I may _ever_ reach you
Despite your toil, your shame.

No sin can separate us 4
No fear can hold us back,
No gate of Hell can close you,
Fear _nothing_ of attack.

For long the battle's over
The victory's been won,
My love will live forever
In the person of My Son.

My gift for you for always,
My life for you alone, 5
That always you will know Me
And call Me for your own.

For often I have called you
And sought you by your name
That hopefully you'd seek Me
And step out from your shame.

The days you know are numbered
And must come to an end,
Decided now for all time,
As homewards now we wend.

*Jesus

Before all time began, I know
I called you by your name,
That now -this day - you'd hear Me call
And turn away from shame.

No sin can separate us
No lie can hold us back
No guilty conscience ever has 6
A right way of attack.

My love will last forever
And now, to you, this day
I give My life again, for good,
I want to hear you say:

"Yes, Lord, take me, I am yours,"
And reach out with your arms
And then I'll come to you and heal
the weight of life's false charms. 7

I'll gently show you My ways,
I'll lead you through the part
Which brings you directly
Deep into My heart.

So only trust My life, My friend,
And seek it for your own,
And then you'll know the peace which comes
From finally coming home." 8

*The name JESUS means 'the Lord saves'. *"In all things know My name"* means to put His name where it is not; for example, in the middle of fear, or worry, or sickness, or disaster, or attack, etcetera, as well as gratefully in happiness, celebration, achievement and so on. Remember Him in <u>all</u> things. If we do this, we bring <u>salvation</u> in to the situation.

'Salvation' means: the act of saving; the means of preservation from any serious evil; the saving of man from the power and penalty of sin; the conferring of eternal happiness.

(There is a background story to this piece in the JOURNAL section.)

18 March 1989   2.30pm

<u>'DIARY' COMMISSION</u>

*"Stop!   Take up your pen and write...*1

My words - to give, to share, as a book to be called

'Diary of the Lord' to be published by

...... & 2

as part of their new section of Religious

publishing."

Tuesday 19 September 1989

"GIVE..ACT IN LOVE"

"Giving, and acting in love, are the keys to the Kingdom of Heaven within you.

The sacred heart of Jesus is a torch that lights the path of all mankind. To those who find this path and enter upon it, much love will be given - Love which is to be shared and poured out as a blessing upon all mankind.

None must be refused who ask of this God-given love. No demand must be curtailed; no sacrifice announced. For in such as these, My heart beats. 1

The lowly are My kingdom among you, My princes among men, scattered2 for the well-being of the souls of My people. How else can compassion flourish, except by demands made upon understanding, by claims upon time, by claims upon hearts?

For the longing of My heart is to have My people nurtured, fed, restored to wholeness - and this can only be done in the loving presence of My Son, whose heart I give you.

Long gone is the day when I wished you to hear Me: and now the present time is one of revelation. For I am revealing directly to your heart an understanding of My longing for you to enter My will.

Leave all things to Me that I may cause you to flourish, safe in the bosom of My family and My love.

51

For you belong to Me and the longings of your heart cause mine to yearn for their satisfaction.

I will restore all that the locusts have ravaged in My beautiful world and the greatness of My creation will rise again.

A time will come when the clamouring of your soul will cease and your spirit will find peace eternally.
Until that day comes turn only to Me with problems, for I alone can help. NO other ears can hear, truly, the longings of your heart. Give utterance to Me alone and in all things other keep your peace.
For I will unburden you. I will release you. I will receive the load you carry. For I have placed within you a steadfast spirit, true to My Precious Name, and I will bless you for this.
The longings of your heart are well known to Me and I hear the clamour of your call.

Know that I am anointing you. Know that I am receiving you. Know that I am blessing you with a steadfast heart which will hold you in times of trouble. You will remain close to Me at all times and none of life's stones will shake you loose.

I AM COMING and the time is at hand to make ready the way of the Lord.

Be at peace - let nothing disturb you. Your place is assured in My Kingdom, where peace and love and joy await you. For so long you have battled and I say unto you -
'Be at peace and know Me as your Lord, for I have secrets to tell you, reserved for My followers'.

Why else would I call you by name? I do want to spend time with you and would like you to spend time with Me.

I have given you <u>all</u> that you need to lead a <u>fruitful</u> life for Me and I shall call it forth in due time. It is alright for you to enjoy life and be less watchful. For I can, and shall, look for you, alerting your eyes at the right and necessary times.

For I am placing within you a **tear of joy** to be shed at My coming. **You will see Me arrive** and My train shall fill the temple of the hearts of My people.

Do not seek to understand **these words** with your mind - rather, they **depend on revelation knowledge, to be received,** and **this only comes through <u>prayer.</u>**
<u>Be prayerful.</u>

Know Me at **<u>all times</u>** through the power and pleasure of prayer. Commune with my Spirit that I may better share with you the longings of **<u>My</u>** heart. <u>Then</u> <u>you</u> will <u>know</u> the discernment of My Spirit within you and your prayers for this will be answered.

Only in prayer can My Spirit come and touch you, and release you, and cause you to come into that place, that haven, of longing for which you yearn and seek Me.

Hear My words. Let them sink deeply into you that the founding of the Word takes place.

I am placing within you a hunger for My Word, made flesh, and in print. These two will feed and nurture you equally and without these, you will surely die - of thirst and of hunger.

Fulfil your needs by **<u>daily</u>** watering of My Spirit through prayer, and by **<u>daily</u>** feeding of My Word, in print, and flesh where possible.[3]

53

*For I am calling you to a new life. The old must pass away and make way for **contemplation**. In the depths of your being, I will create a stirring, a longing, satisfied only by Me.*

And I will come to you. In the depths of your heart I will come to you and make My home.

Make ready the harbour of the Lord.

Attend to My suffering world and lift it, with outstretched hands in supplication, to Me, the Lord; for then I can touch, and heal, and restore, and make new, all the things of the world that need My touch and My presence.

Know Me as Lord and acknowledge Me before others, that the glory of the Lord may fall upon you, may shine before others - and sinners and saints may find Me as their Lord, too.

All glory to Me, before nations, before Man, before false gods, that I might blemish the sullied past, 4 and set the future free to be revived and blessed by Me, for My great glory."

Tuesday 7th November 1989 8.30pm

"A DAY OF ANOINTING...TAKE MY LOVE TO PRISONERS"

"Blessed are they who comfort the afflicted in My world. The running sores of the nations are poverty, disobedience and rebellion. Greed is an added pusillanimous poison.

My deeds are known throughout the world and My signs and wonders abound and yet My people do not know Me. I am calling to nations in a new voice, in a voice of woe 1 bringing tidings to the earth of great joy. For in this day and age a new longing will arise in the hearts of My people to seek their Lord. And I shall be there, waiting.

Go into the nations and spread My word. Let the curse of poverty be driven from My lands - the poverty of spirit which enmeshes people and stops them from beholding their inheritance. Have I not provided? Am I not a God of abundance? Of blessing?

What else then must I do before My people hear ME? Must I cause nation to fall upon nation, warring like dogs? Must I bring punishment and retribution to <u>all</u> the sinners? Can people not learn by the mistakes of others? Must <u>all</u> nations be decimated by plague and violence and greed before they turn to Me for help, for assistance, for love?

Oh, how My heart aches to give them love. I would pour balm on the wounds of their afflictions. I would cause worldly power to cease and usher in a time of great peace, if only My people would turn to ME.

And I mean those I have already called by name. I mean those who profess already to know ME. Many don't, although they use the right words. Few allow Me to touch them, to enter into their hearts. Fewer still obey My words to them. Almost no-one loves Me in return.

*For a day of anointing is at hand and My Spirit will **blow** through the nations. All not rooted in Me will be uprooted and tossed aside in the path of the Spirit's reckoning.*

The wind will blow where it will and no-one will be able to predict. I will separate and pluck brother from brother and only the truthful and righteous will stand. Only those rooted in ME will continue to grow in My presence. All else will pass away.

Intercede for others that I might bless them. Do not think that prayer goes unanswered, even quick, short prayers. All petitions to bless others pass to Me, by My Spirit, and My greatest desire is to bless My people. It is no hardship to open My storehouse and give of My bounty.

*In times of famine people ask freely of Me; but many do not know they are starving. **LOVE** is what they need. It is what they lack. Without it their actions and their prayers are useless, fruitless and barren. Devoid of love, people rest on truth and righteousness. It is not enough.*

*Only **LOVE** informs, excels, upreaches, encourages and inspires. All teachers, without love in their hearts, yield part knowledge.*

Love causes love to flow. Nothing heals better. Power is never greater than when exercised in love, in true gentleness

- not in the gentleness of manner that is adopted by many. Only love yields the fruit, ripens the harvest, secures the crop. Only **MY** love will join nations in brotherhood. Only My love releases captives and prisoners, where prison bars still contain them.

Take My love to the prisons, to the prisoners. Yield to Me a nation₂ of free men, captive only in body, not in spirit. Take My words to the nations and be uplifted of ME.

In the day of anointing a tumult will arise, causing rivers to burst their banks, and many will be swept away on tides of ignorance and prejudice.

All things will come to an end. All chaos will lift and order will be restored.

Rest only in My Spirit and know the peace of My presence within you. Sit and watch My hand on the nations. I will quell the rioters; I will bring peace and healing to troubled minds; I will restore peace and order in the nations; and then you will know the day of MY coming is very near.

The time of peace will usher in a new era, of thanksgiving and gratitude - and My Heart will be uplifted by the praise of contented hearts. Be among My chosen people at this time and wholeheartedly praise Me, in all things, in all areas, in all ways - and know Me as your God for all time.

For I hold you in the palm of My hand, precious of My heart, and My love abounds for you. It knows no limits, not even in your understanding. Be of good faith and know Me, as I know you - wholeheartedly."

Friday 29 December 1989   11.15pm

"PURIFY YOURSELVES...ATONEMENT"

Come! Come to the Lord's feast and enjoy the peace of His suffering, endured by many.
For many have fallen by the wayside and many more, still, seek His anointing. His hand is upon the nations and He will usher in a time of peace, if only His people will turn to Him.
How He longs for His people. How Israel laments for the loss of its sheep.

"Despite the ravages of war, I will prevail," says the Lord. "Nothing will put asunder the covenant of My promise to redeem My people. For I have chosen, I have called by name, and deaf ears are opening. Rejoice at My coming - it will be soon. And nation will cease warring with nation. Famine will cease and the skirts of My peace will cover the land.

*I will put aside all instruments of war and My people shall rise up. I am forming and calling a mighty army to Myself and I will heed the cries and calls of My anguished followers. Many will seek Me but **only the pure will find Me.***

PURIFY YOURSELVES. Be stripped of the world's offerings. Be made whole in My sight by atonement for sins. Repentance is the key and atonement is the place of respite. Within the walls of atonement, perfect peace prevails.
When one heart seeks to comfort Mine, for such is atonement, then My tears will purify and wash clean the souls of the departed.

58

Many languish in Hell for the want of love to release them. My Heart is full of their need and My people need to be made ready to rescue them. A prayer will do. A seeking, earnest, heartfelt plea to My Heart for succour and comfort, will secure the release of a trapped soul₁

Without love nothing moves; nothing heals; nothing is eternally secure. Only love guarantees these things. Seek Me often. Seek My heart for the outpouring of My love to wash away the grime of past years.

Whole lives can be made new, renewed, revitalised, commissioned for growth - if only My people will love, will seek My teaching, will live My words.

Be amongst those who cry 'Holy! Holy is the Lamb, the Lord of Hosts' and I will anoint you with great blessing. Tumultuous outpourings of My Spirit will follow you and the signs and wonders you seek will abound. Share My word with My people. _Tell them who I Am_ - that I Am the Lord who _saves,_ who _heals,_ who _ministers,_ who _releases,_ who _restores,_ who makes _whole;_ and that it is _My pleasure_ to do these things and bring the gift of _Life,_ in _abundance_ and _fullness_.

Tell My people it is not My will that they are prisoners of the mind, or of the body. It is not My will that they perish in a sea of uncertainty, or confusion, or insecurity, or doubt.₂

I Am the Lord, who sets people free. Only I can do these things. Their own efforts and investigations can only take them so far and will always fall short. For completeness - **seek Me**. For wholeness, knock on My door. For health of mind and body, invite Me in.

59

For I alone Am Holy and the holiest people on earth are as base metal.

I shimmer like the sun with the Glory of God. I _am_ the Sun and Glory of God. My name is Jesus, Lord of Lords, eternally begotten of the Father.

I saw you in the mind of My Father before breath was given to your body. Even then I saw your beauty and recognised your belonging to Me. For I alone love you perfectly. Seek no other but Me and all else will come to you.

Be anointed of Me and be made holy. Turn to Me often with love in your eyes and I will give you love in your heart which will heal yourself and My broken world. Go in My name and tell others of Me, for I am their salvation too. I belong to all mankind, to all who invite Me in. I never refuse an open and willing heart. I enter and make My home in the darkest of dwellings, bringing light and wholeness to restore and heal and make whole.

Of _My_ Kingdom, there is no end. Enter in and receive My love, My blessings, My hopes for the world - and your heart will lift and lighten. Be made whole in Me and My love will flow and restore you, make you whole. Surrender your burdens and cast them upon Me, that I might shoulder your cares and replace them with My joy - a perfect gift to bring perfection into My broken world.

Enjoy Me, enjoy My presence.
Call Me Holy and I will call you blessed."

JOURNAL*

*Extracts from '<u>FREED TO BE TENDER</u>' - the journal of
'*DIARY OF THE LORD*'

The following story is the background to the message of
'HOPE' *29 January 1988*.
It is a truly extraordinary demonstration of the way God uses the
intermingling of people's lives to bring about His purposes.
Reading 'HOPE' again within the setting will complete the story.

JOURNAL

Re. *'HOPE' 29 January 1988*

This is an account of the profound love of amazing God who
knows and so cares about the quality of the everyday lives of
ordinary people that He broke in to a South of England prayer
group and offered them healing.

He showed clearly that He was aware of their troubles, difficulties
and deep personal needs and gently encouraged them to receive
His healing. They did respond - to their joy and His glory. What
He did then, for them, He does now for all of us.

THE DREAM - AND THE PRAYER GROUP

I was woken around 1.15am 29 January 1988 from a nightmare
about my young son, by my own wailing and intense pain of
reaction experienced within the dream.

In the dream, for some reason, I had left my 5 year-old L in D's
care; (*D is my treasured friend, but only my husband or my visiting
Mum were the minders of my young sons if I went out.*).
The radio was on and I could hear a broadcasting of a small boy
making an emergency call from a phone box. He had already
explained that he'd been taken in a car somewhere and had
described how he had been sexually 'hurt' by a man, and was
asking plaintively *"Could you help me, please?"*. His live call was cut
off as he was discovered by the abductor while making it; and the
news presenter sent out an impassioned plea for public assistance.

I almost fainted as I recognised L's little voice and the truth I

63

could hear and feel in his plea.

In the rapid quest that followed, I found a stricken D saying that she'd left L with another friend, less well known to me, just for a while - and it turned out that that person's partner had taken L out for a drive. At this point of turmoil, the dream ended.

The pain and fear of this was so awful that I began to agonise in my sleep. My agonised dream wailing became real and loud and woke me from the vivid nightmare. It also woke my husband; (nothing usually wakes him, because he is substantially deaf). I told him briefly and he went back to sleep while I went downstairs to make myself a cup of tea.

Once in my rocking chair (my prayer place), and in tears, I prayed for all children being sexually abused at that moment; and afterwards I prayed for their mothers and families. Then the Lord quietly and slowly said:

"But...do...you...love...the.....abusers?
.....because I do."

His words stopped me in my tracks, almost physically took my breath away. He was acknowledging the sin, yet loving the sinner.

I had previously worked with children who had been deeply damaged and disturbed by adult abusers, often family members. I found the idea of sexual abusers of children so overwhelmingly abhorrent that I really wanted to have nothing to do with them, to the extent of not even allowing them into my thoughts. I had a very high, defensive barrier.

But, because of what the Lord had just said, I realised then that I could not leave the abusers out of the prayer. I did not welcome that understanding, or the choice that was being offered. I could sense Him waiting, very patiently and unconditionally, almost as if He wanted to see what I would do.

I knew I had complete liberty, with no waiting criticism or recrimination. There was no right or wrong decision, just free choice. But He had just shown me <u>His</u> path - of love. I felt I could not bear to lose sight of Him and be left behind, if He was walking that way, no matter how awful I found it.

So, after a few moments struggle I replied "I find that so hard, Lord, but I'm willing to try."

I prayed then for abusers of children; and found that the action became somehow parallel to my emotional antipathy. It was neither easy nor difficult. At the end of praying, my attitude to child abusers had somehow become infused with some softening but no endorsement. It was still wrong, but I was without the stiffening or burden of previous judgement; or the need for continuing defensiveness.

Then He took me completely by surprise and gave me the following list of people and areas of healing.

- *Someone troubled by a sexual assault on a child.*
- *Someone suffering great fatigue.*
- *Someone suffering depression, coldness of response to children, husband.*
- *Someone has suffered through being let down by a mother(parent?) and may still need to forgive.*
- *Someone who has suffered neglect by her husband, in a thoughtless self-seeking way. No deliberate hurt intended, just oblivious to his wife's needs, caused by his own experience of being drained. Forgiveness is needed and a revising of her expectations of her husband. He cannot meet her needs only and it is unrealistic of her and destructive of him to make him feel he ought. Only Jesus can meet <u>needs</u>, especially in a marriage where our only concern is to love our spouse into freedom to grow in love themselves.*
- *Someone has suffered from the demands of sick and sleepless children and is drained right out. The Lord wants to restore your being and refresh you.*
- *Someone has been experiencing a recurrence of negative*

65

behaviour involving how they deal with others, especially when under stress themselves, which they believed the Lord had already changed for good. He has. Reject false guilt. Stand on the truth of your healing and ask the Lord to restore you, and all those people, in His love. Just apologise to them and so release them.

- *Someone suffers pain, terror and oppression to breaking point, drowning in emotional pain which becomes physical, possibly in the form of nightmares - and possibly these are about sexual assault - which are so severe that the person wakes up, gasping for breath, eventually sobbing and crying. Disoriented then for considerable while.*
- *Someone with arthritis in wrist, back, right leg pain..*
- *Someone has been comfort eating and getting caught up in a furtive guilt syndrome.*

The Lord wants to heal you all -now."

I had never received anything like this and I felt stirred up by it, so I sat for a moment, wondering what all this middle-of-the-night affair was about. Then, in a familiar way that soothed and settled me, He dictated again from my heart, giving me the words of **'HOPE' 29 January 1988.**

Afterwards, I became too tired to take it in, so I left it all and went to bed at 3.30am, knowing that I needed to be up again at 6am with a very long day ahead, including a commitment in the evening. When I got up, I was not unduly tired and I was not surprised, because that seems to be how it is when God works. My prayer group leader was teaching 'Life in the Spirit' seminars to another group in a city along the coast; and she liked to take me with her sometimes, so that I could learn.

Tonight would be the session on Baptism in the Spirit. During the journey there, I related the extraordinary events of the previous night/early hours, wanting her advice on what to make of it. She did not comment, but surprised me by insisting I was to read the

66

list and the *'HOPE'* message to the group.

I was nervous at the prospect, because I did not know anything about the people at the prayer group or have any idea who the list referred to; and I'd never received anything like this before. God might have given me the list, but He had stopped there. T offered no explanation, but was very certain that she wanted me to share, so I agreed to do as she asked.

THE PRAYER GROUP.

After the praise and worship I spoke to the group, introducing the list of descriptions by saying that the Lord had given it to me in the middle of the night; but I didn't mention the dream. I added that if anyone felt that a little part might be for them, then please come and say at the end, so that we could pray for them and they could receive their healing from the Lord.

My heart was thumping in my chest so loudly that I could hear it, as I read the list. I then offered and read the words of *'HOPE'* (read again here) as a gift from the Lord.

All this took a little time. The silence and stillness that followed was like a blanket, full, heavy and soft.

After a few moments a man came up to me and whispered that he recognised himself in one of the descriptions. He wept as he related painful relationship difficulties with his father. While I prayed almost silently in tongues, he forgave his father and was released from the burden he'd carried for so many years. His smile and his immediate relaxation transformed him.

Then someone else came, and another, and another. I think T and I prayed with almost everyone in the group, as one after another they confided the personal relevance of one of the descriptions. Finally, the last, older, lady came up to me.

She could barely get the words out:
"I am the person whose child was sexually assaulted - and I've never told anyone. It was over twenty years ago."

67

Her words were like a blow to my heart and stirred up the pain from the dream again. She buckled into my arms, sobbing, and I wept with her, unable to imagine how *she* must feel, because for her it was real. As I held her, the Lord himself dealt with her burden of concealed pain; all I had to do was keep out of His way, while He allowed me to experience a great and marvellous mystery at work.

Later, I shared my dream experience with this newly radiant lady. She realised then that her healing was not coincidental, or accidental, and that God had designed and chosen the specific opportunity for her; and we both had a glimpse of how much God loves us and cares about our individual and personal situations.

Extract from "FREED TO BE TENDER' (journal to 'DIARY)

The following stories are the background to
'LOVE CALL' 21 February 1989.
They show how **God's love** flows through time, place and
people, in a continuous stream. What appears as one thing, for one
reason, reappears at another time, in another place, connecting and
healing people and circumstances through the golden thread of His
purposeful grace.
The thread first appears, in this account, in a song by an American
singer/song writer, which triggers preparation for a Renewal
meeting in the South of England, in 1989. It then loops through
lives and places, weaving connections; and will interlace with
today's reader, whose own response will automatically update this
account.

JOURNAL

Re. 'LOVE CALL' 21 February 1989
Last October (1988) I shared something at Thursday prayer group,
an understanding that the Lord had given me in response to a line
from a Don Francisco song - **"Love is not a feeling - it's an act of
your will"**. The prayer group leader asked me to share about God's
love at the coming Day of Renewal in April.

I have been seeking the Lord about this since, waiting on Him
and hoping He would tell me what He wants. Getting free time
alone, when I'm awake, seems almost impossible; except for 2
hours on a Tuesday evening after the boys have gone to sleep and
before my husband returns from badminton. But I *have* been
blessed frequently when I'm doing the washing-up! I'm really
happy to do it on my own after dinner, because P and the boys are
usually happily playing before bedtime - and I get opportunities to

bathe in whatever the Lord pours out. I wish I knew what happens, but I can only describe it. It feels like a gentle rain of thoughts and insights being poured over my head. They're very beautiful, but sprinkle too fast to remember, especially for me! I don't even know if they go in anywhere! I've just been asking Him to help me remember, because some of them seem so relevant to the coming talk I'm supposed to be giving.

Anyway, today is Tuesday, P has gone to badminton as usual and I settled into prayer again. I have to say that setting this precious Tuesday slot aside to prepare for the Renewal has been a straight choice between my favourite TV programme 'Spender' with Jimmy Nail - and the peace to watch it! - and necessity. Bit hard at the beginning, but very quickly worth it, as it feels now like coming to a familiar and welcoming place.

But tonight was *very* different. I just knew, as I was praying, that I had to stop because there was something to take down from the Lord. Very quickly, and as fast as I could write, He dictated seventeen rhyming verses, beginning with **"Love is like a flowing stream"**.

I've never seen anything like it and I *know* - THIS is for the Renewal in April.

It is a **'LOVE CALL'**.

Thursday 30th March 1989   Park Place Pastoral Centre

Today is Holy Thursday and, as schools have broken up and my husband is on holiday too, I've booked into Park Place for the day and overnight. I need the family-free space to try and break open these words, ready for the Renewal on Saturday. I want to try and find the Scriptural references that must underlie authentic words from God and base the talk on them.

It is the beginning of the Easter Triduum today and the place is full of people who have come to celebrate Easter here, so not as quiet as I'd imagined, but still peaceful and a good place to study.

70

Tonight is the long Mass of the Lord's Supper which includes the washing of feet, followed by the waiting and watching vigil. I haven't done this since my Nan took me to church as a little girl, but it feels wrong to ignore the unexpected opportunity in the same building.

Removing a whole evening will make a difference to the available study time though.

Later

It has taken me **three** hours using my Concordance to track all the Scriptural references to Love, Water, Freedom, Sin, Fear and coming to the Lord that the FIRST verse holds!

And **another three** hours to get as far as Joy and Peace and Purity in the third line of the SECOND verse! I can't handle all this noted information or attempt to present it to people on Saturday. That would just be like a lecture and that's not the right way to go. It's not a classroom situation. If it were, I'd feel more confident. As it is I feel clueless and without tangible preparation.

I've now run out of time if I want to go to Mass. That means the end of the study time too, in real terms, because I have to go home tomorrow - Good Friday.

All I've got for Saturday is the poem the Lord gave me and a few bits from last October. Ten minutes talk at the most. I really hope the Holy Spirit will step into this yawning space and tell me what to do. I've never been so unprepared for anything.

After midnight.

About half an hour before 7.30pm Mass, in the corridor outside the chapel, I met a man wearing a surgical collar and got into conversation. I felt sorry for him and told him the following story* of how, last year, the Lord had healed fused vertebrae in my neck (whiplash from the 1980 car crash) after American evangelist Jim Sepulveda had challenged me.

Jim Sepulveda was listening to the Holy Spirit and asked for

71

the three people suffering from arthritis of the spine to raise their hands. No third person responded and he kept asking. I knew I had arthritis in my neck, but my brain must have been asleep because I didn't think neck=spine. Then my heart began to pound and I thought "Oh - it CAN'T be me."

He kept asking, gently encouraging and inviting the missing person to respond. Eventually, he said that he could not continue with the meeting because the Holy Spirit had said there was a third person; and without that person, things could not proceed. That's when I realised it could possibly be me so, after another long wait, I tentatively raised my hand. He thanked me and called all three of us out to the front, to stand about fifteen feet away from him below the stage he was standing on.

He hadn't called people forward before in the meeting or I would never have put my hand up! This was my first specific healing meeting; (everything else had been within Renewal circles, quiet, gentle, unobtrusive - and I didn't know what to expect). Anyway, having held everything up for everyone, I felt I had no choice except to go with the others and I felt so embarrassed because I'm not naturally a down-the -front person, even for my own benefit.

Jim Sepulveda spoke to each of us in turn. Finally he spoke to me and extended his arm and pointed his finger at me. "Will YOU say "Jesus has healed you"?" he boomed. That took my breath away because, although I had seen some healing elsewhere before then, I had only been able to talk in terms of "He/She/They were healed" and even "I was healed". I didn't KNOW how healing happened and I would not attribute until I knew the truth. But no-one else knew the difficulty I had with this, except God Himself. I KNEW this was the Lord speaking to me through Jim Sepulveda, so I replied "Yes, I will". Jim then said "Receive your healing, in the name of Jesus."

Although I was at least fifteen feet from him and on a lower level, as he spoke and held his hand up towards me, I fell to the

72

floor. I lay on my back for about twenty minutes, unable to get up, as though I was under a heavy invisible blanket. I was peaceful and happy and aware of what was going on at a distance. When I could get up, I had complete movement restored to my neck where there was previously about 45 degrees in either direction. I didn't need my surgical collar again or any more traction at the hospital, because Jesus healed me.*

The man outside the chapel was touched by the testimony and I said that if Jesus healed me, He would heal him - because what He does for one, He offers to all. I offered to pray for the man, who accepted with interest but without real belief. I simply praised and thanked Jesus for what He'd done for me and asked Him to do the same for this man, for His glory. **

**(Five months later I received a letter from this man. He lived miles away along the coast, but he had remembered my Christian name and the name of my church. It's a big parish and he didn't have much to go on, but he persisted in searching for me. Eventually someone suggested I might be the person he wanted. His letter was full of excitement. Within days of the prayer, he was certain that the Lord had completely healed him too! Consequently, he had renewed his faith and was actively involved in an evangelism programme in his parish)

Good Friday 1.30am.

The Holy Thursday service was wonderful. I have never had my feet washed by anyone, much less a priest, and I was weeping before he reached me. Something profound happened to me - but I don't know what.

During the vigil after the service, I was aware of a woman kneeling several rows in front, on the other side of the church. Something about the way she knelt indicated deep unhappiness to me; so when she arrived later in the kitchen as I was making a bedtime drink, I was ready to listen - and she then asked me to pray. I'm not used to praying for people outside a prayer group, but it's great to see God touch them - helps me to pass through my nervous barrier – and see faces change, soften, smile again. Love it!

Good Friday 10am.
Wish I could stay but P and boys expecting me. Not panicking about tomorrow, but in a state of nervous anticipation. Really hope the Holy Spirit shows up or I'm truly sunk!

Saturday 1st April 1989
10am - Today is also All Fools Day; and five years ago today I had my full-immersion baptism. Does that make me a fool for the Lord, I wonder?

'LOVE CALL' to the Portsmouth Renewal at 2pm.

8pm - WHAT A DAY!
Arrived at the Renewal early, having fasted and prayed, but still with no idea what I would say. Feeling full of butterflies. When it was my turn to speak, I told people about the poem that the Lord had given for them and that I would read it and hope that He would give me His words to follow. After I read it I asked the Holy Spirit to please lead, to please give me what He wanted to say. There were some moments of waiting silence that felt like hours - **and then He did!**
The whole thing was electric as I 'broke open' the poem. Words came...measured, clear, concise;
(As anyone would say - Obviously not me, at all!)
I closed by reading the poem again.

People came up for prayer and there was a lot of inner healing – and then an alarming request from an elderly lady to pray for her arm. I was really daunted, because my first thought was *'Not me, Lord - not physical healing'*; but then I realised that she was not asking me to *heal* her, just pray for her. I could do that, so I calmed down. I barely touched her arm, skimming her skin. There was no visible sign of damage, but her arm and hand were stone-cold and white, like marble. I didn't ask her any questions, just very gently supported her arm with one hand and touched her very lightly with the other.

I had the strangest sense that my fingers were like X-rays. Although I could see nothing and I was <u>barely in contact</u> with her, my middle three fingers rested on the skin of her forearm and each finger could each feel /'see'/detect a hard lump in her arm. I just prayed in tongues.

The Lord told me twice to tell her He was <u>so</u> pleased with her faith. When I did, she beamed and said, *"Oh, yes, I <u>do</u> believe, I <u>do</u> believe."* So I repeated His message and then moved on to pray for someone else.

Half an hour later, the lady came back to me, waving her now splinted arm and excitedly crying *"Feel my arm! Feel my arm!"*

She was now wearing a leather-covered, aluminium and latex splint, with the flat side covering her inner forearm and three straps securing it on the outside. Her previously icy hand was now warm, with normal skin tone. The splint was also warm and, at the place where my fingers had 'seen' the lumps in her arm, the splint was positively hot, with the heat 'pouring' down her arm!

I was astonished and asked her what had happened. She then told me that a badly set fracture had stopped the blood circulation in her arm and that she was due to be admitted into hospital two days later for corrective surgery.

The lady was a first-time visitor to the Catholic Renewal from an Anglican community; and she went home, removed the splint, began using her arm again and went to her church the next day and showed her vicar that Jesus had healed her. No more treatment.

A physical miracle! I got to see it at close quarters and it is <u>so</u> completely reassuring to <u>know</u> that none of it had anything to do with me. She had the healing, but I had the Master Class.

Easter 2000

We have been living in Pembrokeshire fifteen days.

I don't know anyone in this town and, as I can't stop crying even when I'm walking the streets, how long will it take to find anyone to talk to?

And I'm missing L so much, it physically hurts. I know his 'A' Levels won't take long, but <u>this</u> separation from him has scooped my heart with a melon baller. P and A miss him dreadfully too.

We're on the run from the Hampshire murder and the looming trial; but, even more than that horror, I am stunned. Mam was found dead three weeks ago. She is supposed to be <u>here</u> in the new house. With us. A new life, <u>all</u> of us, <u>together</u>. This is a bottomless, airless pit.

Five days later.

Today a letter arrived from a lady who had been at the *'LOVE CALL'* meeting all that time ago in 1989. The talk had been audio taped and she had just listened to it again. The Lord had newly ministered to her in a beautiful, healing way, so she was giving a copy of the tape to her church library and wanted to let me know. It has taken her weeks to track me down, but her letter arrived in the nick of time for me.

It brought a tiny ray of sunshine that let me know I was not completely dead. I felt gently lifted up and I knew it was <u>Him</u> telling me I was not lost or forgotten, no matter what I felt. I wept with relief and gratitude and blessed Margaret for her efforts to reach me. I was beginning to think I had imagined Him, that He belonged to another life, another mind, a different person. But I still don't know where I am, who I am, or who He is any more. And right now, I don't much care.

P.S. September 2008

The previous dark night of the soul is not a place to end this account, because everything changed - as everything must. Love flows where it will, mercifully not needing our permission, washing turmoil with it.

It was a time of sojourn that God alone brought me through. I can see now that it was a place of laying down my life. Completely. In every way.

During the first six months, if I could have found the 'off' button, I would have pressed it. Not to kill myself – because in a strange way, living and dying felt like the same thing to me at that time – but to stop any more emotional life coming through me.

I was too angry with God to pray or read Scripture, untrusting of any more words between us. But He had a better, new way of communicating with me, already waiting.

After the murder of our next-door neighbour in the south of England, He quickly led us to the most beautiful part of the country, to a house on spectacular coast. *Every* time I walked the two hundred metres to the end of my road and looked across the short stretch of sea to Caldey Island, my stomach would literally drop at the beauty of the view. Inadvertently, over the year, I began to relax and He began to communicate with me through His creation, soothing me with beauty, washing me with silence. Hidden country lanes banked with purple and white violets. Vast lily ponds leading to a sunny cove. Stormy nights and crashing waves reminding us how wonderfully small we are in the face of creation.Walking the moonlit beach at midnight, safely alone. Time.

Like a loving parent cradling a sick child, the Lord spoon-fed me new life. Many small kindnesses from old and new friends brought some sweetness - until I was well enough to recognise that it was unforgiveness about the murder, laced with fear and hatred, that was poisoning me with a broth of bitterness.

Tender ministry from a blind priest who could not read my body language, but challenged me to my core, opened my spiritual ears to the crucial importance of dealing with fear – then helped me undermine it's strength in my life, by leading me in repentance for my harboured sin. I think he saved my spiritual life.

Afterwards, I could receive love again – and hopefully begin to give it. I have <u>lived</u> the truth of '*LOVE CALL*'.

DIARY of the LORD

CONTENTS 1990 – 99

10.35am Wednesday 15th August 1990

"I DO PRESIDE"

"Behold, the day of the Lord's anointing is fast approaching. Before your eyes, and before the eyes of men, will come a tumultuous outpouring of My Spirit. Valleys will ring with the shouts of the voices of My people. Praise will ascend to the mountain tops. Lions will lie down with lambs upon the green countryside and the world will be turned upside down.

Before the dawn of the Redeemer's coming, many will tremble with anticipation. Loss of many things will incur disbelief in the eyes and hearts of My followers - for how could their Lord preside over these things, over such desolation and destruction? 1

But I do preside. I will preside. I will be seen to be a God of the anointing, before whom all things must pass away, for the new order to be established.

Be among those who stand firm. Comfort My followers and soothe their fears. My hand is on the nations and these things must come to pass, in order to usher in a new time of belonging to Me.

For I alone am Holy; I alone speak the words of redemption. Do not heed the words of prophets who disturb the peace of your heart; for I have given you the peace. It is not complacency, to be challenged. It is peace, to be restored by My hand, with My voice, in My time.

No longer fear the unknown.

Love all comers with a strength and decision given by Me and blessed by My Spirit.

Be seen to be anointed of Me and let your words be holy.

Be stripped of all not of Me that hinders and dresses your spirit, for the beauty of the bare and naked soul is a vulnerability that shows utmost reliance on Me.

I shall adorn you with garlands of _praise_. I shall anoint you with garments of _thanksgiving._ I shall dress you in clothes of the finest _prayer_.

And these, priceless, will be seen to be fitting.

For in this day of the Lord's anointing, I shall cause mountains to tumble and barriers and defences to break down.

Nothing shall stand in the face of the Lord's coming.

No obstacle shall endanger the spreading of My Word.

All shall bow before Me, starting with you.

My might shall be seen, clearly visible, in the eyes of My people. The brightness of My glory shall shine forth and smite the foe, the Enemy of **_My_** Way.

I shall see to these things. Only let your eyes see and your ears hear. Develop your obedient spirit, unburdened by binding, yet compliant to My will. 2

Let Me mould you and use you.

Be anointed of Me, to endeavour in My ways, to spread My word.

Let the anointing rest upon you and _give thanks to the Lord,_ in _all_ things, at _all_ times."

82

Friday 9 November 1990   10.00am

"I AM THE REFINER...PURIFIED BEYOND PRECIOUSNESS"

Repentance, Forgiveness and Intercession.

"*These are the words for today, for the Day of the Lord. Fast approaching is a tumultuous wave of criticism which will wash the unsteady off their feet. Half hearted interest in me will be washed away and with it the followers who were unable to find room for Me in their hearts.*

Too many hearts have frozen and many are going cold. Indifference has spread and is poisoning the nation. Ignorance is rife and My Heart yearns for My people. They are my people. <u>You</u> are My people.

The Day of the Lord demands a treaty of love, a love to be outpoured on the nations.

See the drums of war beat faster and all who yearn for Me are lost in the beat, trampled on by marching feet of oppression. and unforgiveness. Hatred is unrelenting and stalks the face of My beloved earth. Go and tell the news that I bring to My Creation.

Willing ears must listen.

Willing hearts must receive.

Willing lips must share.

Willing hands must carry the burden I am offering to My people.

My burden is peace, not of the ordinary kind.

83

This peace can only be received by hearts that are willing to change, by hearts which will allow __Me__ to bring the change.

Unless My people are broken, unless My people relent and allow Me to be King in their lives, they will not see the glory of the Lord.
> *It is not enough to pay Me lip-service.*
> *It is not enough to say 'Yes, Lord'.*
> *It is not enough to praise Me.*

I want a people of change, who will allow change in their lives.
> *Comfort belongs to the past.*
The time of change I am ushering in is a time of turmoil, of turbulence, in hearts as well as lives.

No change can take place unless people let go of their longings, their possessions, their hopes, their desires, their wishes, their dreams, their successes, their failures, their hurts, their unforgiveness, their memories, their bitterness, their wrongdoings, their misdeeds, their wrong actions, their wrong exercise of power, their self-willed righteousness (which has nothing to do with __My__ righteousness), their claims of glory, their ambivalence, their fortitude in crisis.
I would have a people stripped of their natural resources, their natural strengths (good though they may be). I want a people of vulnerability, defenceless and naked before Me - that I might bestow upon them a purified heart of longing for Me.

I require restitution of all that I have lost - of all that has been plundered from Me.
> *Only pure hearts can restore Me.*
> *Only pure hearts can receive Me.*

Only pure hearts can love Me.
I am sick of contaminated hearts being raised half-heartedly to Me. Contamination by sin offends Me and lowers the praises of My people. I cannot be praised by hearts that are burdened and weighed down by wrongdoing.

I seek hearts that are willing to relinquish the worldly cares that they carry, for I cannot inhabit hearts that are partitioned in sections.

I require whole hearts where all the corners have been swept clean.

It is not difficult to do, for I can restore in the twinkling of an eye.

I require people to rise up and become of God, seen to be Godly in this world of darkness. How else can I, the Lord your God, reclaim what is rightfully Mine?

Did I not create a world of beauty, of harmony, of peace?

Destruction sickens Me and I need to prepare My people for war.

The war I speak of is in the Darkness, against the darkness. Only vessels of light will be able to help.

I am calling you to be vessels of light.

Purify your hearts.

Relinquish the hold of the world.

Do not be afraid. I will not strip you of the love you know, of the love of family, or of friends. Such I have given you to enhance and protect your lives. What I have given in love, of love, I will not take away.

Rather, learn to know Me for yourself. Each one I call personally to become a warrior in My Kingdom.
And do not feel daunted by the word 'warrior'. Those I call, I equip.

You must repent of old ways. You must repent of time not spent in My presence. You must turn to Me and call Me 'Beloved' that I might purify your heart.
I will fill your hearts with forgiveness. I will create a forgiving world.
Can you imagine that?
Pause for a moment and consider that.

What would you have Me do, to prove My love for you?
My Son has died, at My request.
I have no greater gift.
My life I offer you, freely, without charge.
I ask that you allow My life to <u>change</u> you.

Do not be afraid of change. Growth cannot come without it.
It is time for My people to grow to maturity. It is time that the milk of kindness is replaced by the flesh of the heart.
It is <u>My</u> flesh I feed you with, <u>My</u> heart that is offered to you, for you to become like Me.

The change I ask of you is a willingness to become like Me. I made you in My image and I wish to grow in you.
Be made <u>holy</u>. I need a <u>holy</u> people to walk this earth.
Only holiness will cause the darkness to be driven back.
All will be engulfed except the holy.
They will stand, purified by the Refiner's fire.

I AM the REFINER

*My fire is righteous and burns away unholiness. Purified beyond
preciousness - that is my gift to you, My people.*
> *I call you by name, to follow Me.*
> *Will you allow Me to enter in?*
> *Will you allow Me to love you into wholeness?*
Will you allow Me to abide in you, that you might abide in Me?

> *For I Am the Lord, who calls and seeks you.*
> *Many have been called and not heeded My voice.*
> *Many have ignored Me, leaving Me to another day.*
> *But time is short.*
*There is no place to hide from the scrutiny of the Lord. The King
comes in majesty - awful and mighty.*
> *Know your place before Me.*
> *Bow down in worship.*
Folly has no place in My people - and it is foolish to ignore Me.

*My ceremony is righteousness and this is an age which will be
ushered in.*

I know My people. I long for My people. I need My people.

> *Will you answer Me?"* 2

87

"TAKE TIME..MASTER CRAFTSMAN..."

"Take time – take time to listen and you will feel the tensions ebb away from you.

The heart of purity you seek is being fashioned in My time and in My making.

No longer seek the ways of others. Let all these things fall away from you. 1

I am showing you a new way, never before seen by the eyes of unbelievers.

Into My hands I take the lives of My faithful - and I mould and fashion in My own design. 2

Each pot is perfect and unique when I, the Master Craftsman, yield My work for observation.

Be not afraid and let none intrude on My work. Be not afraid. Do not doubt.

My love for you overflows the vessel, pouring down over the sides, washing the outside clean as well as purifying the inside. 3
***

Step into the anointing, into the new place I have carved out for you; and rest, assured, that I the Lord your God sustain you in your travels through this life; and that I have prepared a place before you, for your coming into My land.

My kingdom belongs to you, child of My heart. Enter in and enjoy My love, for you and yours, this day and forever."

***   The following section is abbreviated and personal, extracted from the body of the piece, but included here because of important learning points - which are dealt with in the **Footnotes** section.

"Do not worry about your husband. He is hearing My voice, although He does not yet recognise it. 4 Honour him in all things and My glory will abound in your house."5

Saturday 21st September 1991 5.40pm

"I AM A PERSONAL GOD..."

"This is the day of the Lord's coming. Hearken ye, My people! Let your minds dwell no longer on the coming war. Instead hasten to the battlements. Citadels will fall and the time to move is <u>now</u>! Be prepared, for all at once a tumultuous clap will rend the Heavens. Be on your guard for this is the sign you are awaiting.

The Lord will come in glory and in judgement and His words will be emblazoned on the foreheads of His followers - "Glory, Honour, Power and Praise, to the Lamb."

The days will be days of amazement and outpouring, when neighbour will seek neighbour and the divide will be breached. No longer will people stand apart, aloof. The searching of the Spirit will cause all to seek wherever they can find and many will be lost, misguided.

Disunity will vanish and My Church will be healed, but this will be after the great Uprising. This uprising will be when My people unite behind ME and not behind men. This movement is beginning. I am calling people out of their cavities into a cavern, so great will be the difference. And the worship will have no end. And the glory will outshine the sun.

Come out of your insular ways, My people.
Come forth, and be disrobed of your grave clothes. 1

90

Leave dying ways for the Way of Truth.
I _Am_ the Truth; the only Way; and Life itself.
Be amongst My followers.
Be amongst My holy and anointed ones.
Be seen to be worthy of Me.
Leave old ways behind.
   There is no other path to Me except the one I lead _you_ on.

I am a _personal_ God.
   I saved _you_.

I do not need you in a service, or a congregation, or a praise gathering, or a worship meeting. ₂

   I need you in the silence of your heart, in the quietness of your soul.
   I need you to meet Me, not gather before Me.
You do not need to wait for Me to come. I have never left you.

Be anointed; rest awhile in My presence. Let My love come upon you and you will know the delights of My heart.
The meanderings will cease. The only path that matters is the path to My heart.
Then, your praise will rise to the heavens.
Then your worship will be worthy of Me.
Until then, rest in the knowledge of My love for you; My love that heals, and soothes, and gentles, and calms. _My_ love, not 'the love of God'. _My_ love.
   _I_ love _you_.

   Do you know what that means?

It means I cherish, I uphold, I strengthen, I confirm, I bless, I release, I soothe, I revive, I exhort, I admonish, I create, I deliver, I heal, I send forth, I commission.
Do you want these things?

And what of the gentler moments, when I take you to Myself,
as a lover?
What of the stilling of your heart to beat with Mine?
What of your breathing My breath, breath of My breath, love of
My love, heart of My heart?
Could I cherish you more? Could I court you more graciously?
I think not.
Come into My arms and learn the new way, the only way worth being.
There is no better place, no easier time, than here and now.

If you will only hear My voice, My people, you will rise up victorious in this land bedevilled by evil. Oppression will cease to matter and struggle will be a by-word for old ways.
The Resurrection is and does not need to be established by 'right' ways or by doctrinal evidence.
You will find it in My heart and nowhere else, although you may glimpse it elsewhere in many places. Why settle for less?
The love of My heart is poured out for you.
The blood of My Son ran for you.
The weeping of My Spirit takes place - for you.

Come again into that place of calling and leave behind old ways.
Hear Me for yourself.
Trust My heart for you.
You are safe and will always be separated from the darkness you

fear. It has no hold and cannot touch you or harm you. You and yours are Mine, and <u>none</u> shall lift his hand against the Lord's anointed. Would I give you less than I gave My Son, whose brothers and sisters you are?

Fear not suffering. Embrace the cross. Survival does not matter. Transfiguration does. Suffering will transfigure you.

Be a suffering people. Become a suffering people. Do not seek or contrive ways to suffer. The suffering <u>I</u> have in mind is already in store for you who wish to follow Me.

It is a suffering of the Spirit and a transforming of the heart. 3 *These things happen each day, in many and little ways.*

Leave the paths of coping and understanding. You no longer need the props.

Learn how to embrace the moment fully, shielding yourself no longer. This is turning the other cheek.

In silence, accept the rebuke, the hostility, the wounding gossip - and forgive. Let the pain of the suffering moment burn like a flame until it dies away, by itself. Do not extinguish it, or soothe it, or be distracted from it. It will not last long. It <u>will</u> cauterise - you will not bleed to any kind of death - rather you will be transformed.

That part of your heart will be, in that moment, forever Mine.

See, I am making new hearts in My people. Burnished hearts of bronze and gold.

No greater armour can be put on.

Those at the battlements need these hearts. No other will survive the onslaught. And these will never again be wounded.

Believe Me, My people.

I know I am calling you into danger, but you must face the enemy without fear and without delay.

> *See, the Armourer is ready, the fire hot.*
> *Step into My heart - and receive yours.*
> *There is no time to lose.*
> *There is eternity to gain.*

Be not afraid. I AM before you. I go with you. I AM at your side.
Forget the past. Change nothing by effort.

> *Just **accept My love**.*

*The rest is up to Me and I am waiting - for **you**."*

Monday 28th October 1991 11.45am

"PRAYER... I AM THE TRUTH AND THE SUCCOUR"

"In the days of the Lord's reckoning, nation will war against nation. Dogs will grip the throats of other dogs and warring and fighting will break out. Fear not, for the Lord's hand is upon the nations.

No nation will cower before the Lord which sings His praises.

No nation need fear His coming, if prayer is in their hearts.

But woe to the unprepared; to those who think it does not matter... For they will be lost.

*Power is in **praise** and **prayer**.*

Power to overthrow thrones and governments.

Praise is the key which unlocks the treasures of My heart.

Prayer is the tool, the weapon, the shield which protects My people's lives.

Without prayer they are nothing.

Without prayer they have nothing.

Without prayer they will not seek Me; they will not find Me. They will not hear Me, or see Me.

Without prayer they are like dry channels of dust.

__With__ prayer, they are like flowing torrents of fresh, clean pure water - revitalising and refreshed.

With prayer they may come to the Father's throne and be sure of a hearing.

With prayer they can subdue nations.

With prayer they can bless their priests.

95

With prayer they can minister to the hungry, the oppressed, the starved (in spirit), the weak, the aimless, the poor.

Without prayer they are useless. They hinder the work of the Kingdom.
With prayer they bless the lives of all they meet.
Without prayer they are barren, devoid of blessing, shadowed and stumbling in the dark.

Prayer brings you into the presence of God.
Prayer allows God to touch your hearts.
Prayer allows Me to embrace and love you, enfolding you to My heart.
Prayer is My gift to you; a special time of closeness and uniqueness when you will hear **My** voice and not the voice of others.
My secrets are revealed in prayer times.
My heart is opened in prayer time.
My love is released and flows, through prayer.

Be among My followers who pray, daily. Seek My face in all things and hear My voice.
I _will_ reveal to you time-honoured truths.
I _will_ show you the goodness of My heart and the richness of My Spirit.
Cast all your fears and doubts away and seek the anointing on your heart; the anointing that comes when My Spirit touches yours.
This happens in prayer times, even if you do not feel it. Believe Me.
I touch, and linger, and hope that My people will turn to Me for their refreshment and succour.
I _Am_ the Truth and the Succour, the vital source of Life.
Be among My fruitful servants. Be faithful to My words.

Be seen to be anointed of Me. Be seen to be My love.
For the anointing is upon you.
Days will seem like years spent in my company, so full will be your experience of Me in the time you give Me.

Take of the time I have given you. Already you have your complete life, a gift from Me.
Take of the abundance of time given to you and share some with Me that I might bless you further.
Experience My blessing at the moment of gift. This I promise you in prayer.
Know that I Am the Lord, your God. Know that I have surrendered, for you, a life so precious to Me. For your sake, I gave Mine. Be it known to you that I love you. Let the words drop into your heart, deeply. Know that I confess you to My Father, preparing a table for the banquet I invite you to.

Be pleased to spend time with Me, that I might change your life.
Be pleased to welcome the Holy Spirit as you enter His domain.
Prayer is the domain of the Holy Spirit.
Grasp it closely to your heart.
Clasp the precious gift I am giving you, as I call you to spend time with Me.

Your whole life is a prayer, if it is released fully to Me, but even more precious is the life I return to you when you pray. That life is cleansed, refreshed, revitalised. As a mechanic tends the parts of a car, keeping them in good running order, so I tend your spirit, strengthening your life. A pit stop is vital in a race - so are spiritual stops in your life.
This is what I am offering and what I am exhorting you to take up.

97

Only then will you see the fruit you yearn for and vainly seek.
Only then will you discern My will for you and for others.
Only then then will you feel the touch of My hand upon your life,
calling you to greater things.

Feed on My Word. Be anointed of Me.
Feed on My Presence. Be blessed By Me.

Be amongst the tender hearted who call Me Lord in the vale of tears.
Prayer will surely soften your heart and tears will surely cleanse it.
Be not afraid of tears in prayer time. They are a sign of My Spirit
and not your madness. Rather you are being changed. Always for
the good. Always by My love.

Come and receive what I offer you.
Come and pray, so that I can talk to you.
Spend time in My presence. Grace Me with your company. Let Me
call you 'Beloved' as I tenderly whisper in your ear the words of
longing I have for you. You will know beyond doubt of My love for
you. You will know beyond doubt that you are safe. You will know
beyond doubt that I live.

Will you come, precious of My heart, and spend time in prayer?
Only then will I be able to comfort you in the way you long for.
Only then can I call you Mine and you will hear. You are Mine
whether or not you hear it, but if you want to hear - spend time in
prayer.

Be with Me, be near Me; wait upon Me that I might bless you.
Be filled with My presence - in prayer."

18th November 1991   12.10pm

"PURITY...I AM THE HARVESTER..THE RESTORER"

"Blessed are those who call upon the name of the Lord.
Blessed are those who seek His face.
Blessed are those who build on the Cornerstone.
Plan your lives, My people, upon the touch of the Lord.
For He alone is the answer to all your needs.

For in these days of outpouring many dreams will be answered.
Many hopes will be lifted up.
For the anointing of the Lord is great; is virtuous; is life-giving.
Seek, often, the outpouring upon yourselves.
The day of the Lord is fast approaching. Fear not. Be among the leaders of My people, of My scattered flock.
Know that in the depths of your heart I will come to you.
Know that I will anoint and bless you. Know that I care for you, deeply.

The stillness of your heart is a delight to Me, an oasis of peace wherein I can spend My rest. For I, too, need to rest awhile - in your company. Tend My heart, which is bruised and tired. Tend, with loving care, the needs of the man who bore you in His arms to His Father. Tend, in the loving company of others, the wounds which bleed profusely in My damaged world.
For you know of these things.
I have given you a heart to tend the wounded, the afflicted, the dis-eased, the grieving, the sorrowful, the depressed, the oppressed.

For love of Me let your tears flow as you tend My wounded.

Look again at <u>My</u> labours, at My <u>wounds</u> and wonder, then, at yours. Are they so terrible, or are they a small price to pay for My pleasure?

It pleases Me to see you work in the way I designed for you.
It pleases Me to see you spend yourself for others, for you are very close to Me and <u>in</u> My heart, at these moments.
<u>Know</u> that I love you. Know that I am waiting for you.

Time spent in My company is never lost, or wasted.
<u>All</u> moments given to Me, shared with Me, bear fruit of such succulence. It is My pleasure to feast on the fruit of your sacrifice.

Sacrifice is a hard word and is <u>not</u> self-<u>denial.</u>
Sacrifice is self-<u>giving</u>. It is making of yourself an offering, as a lamb to the slaughter, as a bunch of grapes in the wine press, as an olive yielding oil. Without the gift there would be no produce.
Sacrifice is a gift, made in love, whatever the cost.
Do not be confused by words, or drawn into semantics.
Discussion will not alter what I say.
Give to Me of your <u>self</u>, even when it hurts.
I will then bless you, to give of your fruitful self to others.
But first, give to Me.
Only then will the gift be pure, pure enough to enlighten the world, its darkness, and ease the pain of others.

Spending a purified Self brings purity into the world.
Purity is a radiance that blinds evil and dispels darkness.
Do not settle for less.
Purity is the cutting edge of My sword of the Spirit.
It blazes towards Heaven, drawing down Heaven's power to dispel

and vanquish the evil hordes that crowd around men, polluting the atmosphere of My creation. 1

I would have a pure world, where symptoms of madness and confusion disappear. 2

I would have a pure world where darkness does not hold sway over the minds of captives.

I would have a pure world wherein I can rest My Spirit, to drink of your waters of purity.

Be not afraid for I, the Lord your God, cover you with the palm of My hand. None shall harm you. All shall benefit from your growth. Bring glory to Me in this, My child. Bring glory to the foot of the cross and offer it to My bleeding Son. His wounds will bleed upon you and you will be cleansed of all, even secret things forgotten.

Be not afraid.

In the going out of this news will come much blessing.

In the receiving of this word will come much release.

In the employment of this word will come a great harvest.

I Am the Harvester, who reaps where others sow.

I am giving you the seed to sow.

Find fallow ground where nothing has grown for a while and sow My seeds. It is ready and fertile and growth will be rapid.

Sacrifice is a gift of the whole person, however broken, damaged, wounded, or small. Self-denial is ... a refusal to give, but many have learned old ways. Tell them of the truth, of the only way to give.

Come to Me, in brokenness of spirit and I will bind your wounds. The comforting arms of others can carry you to Me, but I, alone, will bind and heal. **I, alone, Am the Healer.**

Forget old ways, and old ways of knowing. My truth is all you *need. Seek it with all your heart that knowledge might fall away from you.*

Be seen to seek only Me, to make Me your only Authority. Trust no others. Trust not even those who have seen Me. Trust only Me - and trust Me fully, with every fibre of your being.

> *Trust Me because I AM.*
>
> *Because I give LIFE.*
>
> *Because I AM LIFE.*

I give love in abundance and life without end.

Where else will you find this?

> *Know of the things I am doing by seeking Me, for yourself.*

> *Know of the pleasure I have in you by receiving My Spirit within you.*

> *Seek Me in the sacraments, in My Word, in the stillness of your heart.*

Hear Me for yourself. Test the sound you hear, until you are confident it is I talking to you. Take joy in My Presence and welcome Me, that I might take My rest in you.

Be pleased to spend time in My presence and savour My delights. I bring you gifts of longing and understanding

You will long for Me and will, in time, understand My words.

> *Only remember this....*

There can be no other before Me, in your heart.

A heart given wholly to Me will be a heart that can be a home to multitudes, so fear no loss of your loved ones. There will be no loss or rejection, no displacing. Rather there will be a re-placing, as I take My rightful place in the heart I have chosen.

> *I choose you.*
>
> *I call you.*
>
> *I anoint you.*

102

Receive My call. Receive My Presence. Let My Spirit bless you and render you fruitful.

Be pleased with Me.

Be happy that I call you.

Never mind the world and what it says. Leave old ways behind.

Step into a new way of living.

I AM the RESTORER.

I restore all that has been lost, consumed by fire, or locust. I return, whole, hearts that have been perished by the cold onslaught of winds of changing thought.

I restore straightness to paths made crooked by confusion.

I restore strength where doubt has left weakness in its wake.

I restore happiness to hearts rent asunder by emotions torn and shredded.

I restore wholeness to minds persecuted by evil.

I restore laughter to eyes that have dulled and mouths turned downwards by sorrow.

I restore spirit to dead souls.

I restore life to walking dead.

I bring Resurrection.

I AM Resurrection.

Without Me, nothing lives, grows, hopes, revives.

With Me all life is possible, abundant in fruitfulness, endless in richness and variety.

It is My gift to you.

Take it; share in it; bathe in My Presence.

For I Am sufficient unto you.

You will no longer seek Me without finding - if you feed on My Word.

You will no longer suffer loneliness in the depths of your being - if you feed in My presence.

You will no longer seek the anointing and be left untouched - if <u>you</u> <u>restore</u> <u>Me</u> to My rightful place in your heart.

Put me first that I might confess you to My Father.
Put Me first that My mantle of protection may flow around you and yours.
Put Me first that all honour and glory is given to My Father.

Know that these words are for you.
Know that the day draws near when I, Myself, will come and take you to Myself. I will enfold and love you. I will make you captive in My heart, bound only by love.

I cherish you, I desire you, I yearn for you, Beloved.
Come and rest awhile in My presence and let Me love you.
Let Me show you the way to My heart."

11th December 1991

"I AM THE BRINGER OF HOPE."

"I am the Wounded One, who calls you to sit at My side. I am the Anointed One, who pours blessings upon you. I am the Holy One, the Lord God of Israel.

For too long you have turned away from Me, or not opened your heart properly to Me. I would put this right. Step awhile into My Presence and discover that the love of your life awaits you. For you need seek no further.

The disappointments that have shadowed you, where others have failed to respond, will be wiped away.

The love that I have for you is all seeing. I would never pass you over, could never pass you by. You need fear, no longer, the power of the world to threaten or frighten you. It is not too big for you to live in, even though you feel small. You are only small enough to sit in the palm of My hand. Is there a better size to be? Can you imagine a nicer place to be, or a warmer place to thaw your heart?

Do not worry about your frozen responses.

Love alone will thaw them and My love is safe, and gentle. You will not be hurt again by the disappointment of men if you will gladly take your place in My hand.

Relinquish the cares you carry. The burden is not for you –
it is for ME.
My shoulders are broad while yours are weak and worldly.

The cares the world thrusts upon you are not meant for human shoulders, since their source is more than human.
But I am greater than that source.
Know that I am Almighty, all powerful, all loving, all vanquishing, all safe.
I AM the SAVIOUR....
I AM your SAVIOUR

Will you not take Me into your heart? Will you not allow Me to reside within you? Will you not allow Me to cherish you?
Have done with empty prayers which reach for Me but which do not allow Me entry.
Have done with rituals which allow you the satisfaction of right actions, but which protect you from the need for a response to Me.

Take, instead, the invitation of My heart to welcome you into that secret, private place that I have prepared for you. I know your heart. I know your need for privacy, to keep yourself to yourself. But do not keep yourself from Me.
I await you in the quietness of your heart, if you will permit it.
A meeting could take place which will change your life - if you will allow it.
What have you got to lose?

Is there anywhere else you could go, to find what I am offering you?
Is there anyone else who could succour you so gently, so positively?
What exactly am I offering you?

I am offering you a life of freedom: freedom from self-imposed restraints, self-set standards that are impossible to meet because

106

they are the product of your mind, not the expression of your heart. Can you tell the difference? Would you like Me to show you how to distinguish?

Would you like Me to show you how to step into the difference?

Would you like Me to release you?

I wait upon you with longing in My heart.

I wait upon you with joy in My Spirit.

You are precious to Me and I would travel far to watch and see you. I have travelled with you all your life, a great distance, to rescue you from the oppression which surrounds you.

Oppression surrounds every one, but some are better equipped than others to deal with it and so seem not to suffer as you do. They do, but with strength and love, gained from MY presence in their heart. This I offer you.

Come into a new place, a deeper place than you have entered. Do not be afraid of what you will find.

The innermost secrets of your heart, locked away and shuttered from the gaze of others, are already known to Me - and precious beyond words.

I long to pour balm on your hidden wounds.

I long to pour peace into your soul.

I long to release My Spirit in your heart, so that you, too, will know the JOY of salvation.

Joy is My gift to you. It is all that awaits you. Fear not the troubles of your heart. You will find that if you invite Me in I shall already be awaiting you when you turn inwards to meet Me. I can accomplish in an instant things that can only be dreamed of.

Dream of the peace you long for.

Dream of the power you need.

Dream of the love you hunger for.

Invite Me in and these will be yours for the receiving.

I am the RECEIVER - of all that troubles you, ails you, limits you, binds you, seeks you out to trap you, tempts you, provokes you, angers you, dumbfounds you, blinds you, irritates you, threatens you, worries you - if you will give your heart to Me.

So gently will I change you. It will be My joy to perfect your responses. These things cannot happen without Me. All effort fails to achieve if it is impurely linked or separated from My Spirit.

Together we can achieve the Father's will in your life.
Together we can bring to fruition the promises laid down at your baptism.
Together we can see the fruitfulness of your labour yield a harvest of hope, where bitterness was planted.
Step into the safety of the place I have prepared for you - the safety of My heart.
Let My Spirit soar freely. He will release you and bring you abundant joy.

Let My fingers hush the lips that speak sorrow from your heart and teach you how to smile again: how to smile from a heart restored. The agony of the past is yours, but not to keep. You have held it for so long and now it is time to relinquish it. It was not yours to store, never yours to carry. The burden has been too great for you. Give it now to Me, where it belongs. You will not burden Me, for I have already carried this _and_ disposed of it.
The Cross at Calvary held its weight as well as My suffering body. What was the point of My suffering, if you hold on to yours? I died to set you free - to carry you _through_ your suffering and out

108

at the end. I did not die for you to parcel it up and strap it on your back.

Cast it off and feel the new lightness.

You will not lose the loved ones who are so bound in your suffering. Rather you will release them to Me so that I can, at last, reach them too.

I bring eternal life to all who will receive.

I bring eternal love to all who will receive,

I bring freedom from exhaustion to those who are oppressed by burdens.

I bring freedom from despair to all who walk in sorrow.

I bring light to dispel darkness.

I bring light to bathe in and to walk in.

I am the BRINGER of HOPE.

- Hope to a troubled world, hope to anguished hearts, hope to confused minds, hope to despairing families.

Avail yourself of these gifts. They are for you. The only cost is a willing heart.

Are you willing?

28th March 1992

"I AM LORD"

"Come, My people, be uplifted of Me. For many years I have lain gifts at your feet, showered blessings on your head, anointed your spirits many, many times with My presence.

And what have you done with these gifts, the outpourings of My Spirit?

For some they lie like overlooked presents on dusty shelves - another trophy from the Lord to be dusted and cleaned and admired, but occasionally. And what do you see as you clean this precious silver? Do you see clear reflections of My love, or do you see distorted faces with eyes empty of life? Can you draw sustenance from the reflection? For what you see is what you give.

You are hollow eyed, like famine victims agonising for more food. But I _have_ fed you. I _do_ feed you. _You_ do not feed _others._ For such is My law that it is in _giving_ that you receive. ₁

Unlock the storehouses of My provision. Unlock your lives. Unlock your hearts and _feed_ My starving world. Unless you give of the riches I have abundantly blessed you with, My world will starve and die. Many, many people are lost and wandering, unknowing of which way to turn. I have shown _you_ the Way. Many, many people are starving, searching for crumbs to sustain their meagre life.

_I_ have fed _you_ at a daily feast. _Share_ what you have been given.

The darkness looms and threatens to engulf us all. It is an evil time. But joy is waiting to break through. Laughter will be heard ringing through people's lives, laughter in the middle of great need, if only _you_ will open your heart and let the blessings trickle out.

I do not ask you to stand on street corners and evangelise, as you have seen some do. For most of you this is a fearful thing and I know that. What I call you to do is gently open your heart, so that it is open to everyone you meet, in the shops, at a bus stop, in the hair-dresser's, while you are cleaning your car, in your place of work, in your place of rest, in your leisure place, in your home, in your church   - _especially_ in your church. It is too easy in your church to have hardened hearts, leaving responsibility for others to God. Much reaching out is necessary in church. Many hands must be extended in concern, in friendship, in _real_ interest and care. For if you do not love those who purport to love Me, what do you show the world? What kind of beacon can you be? Division and discord must be healed. Disinterest is a killer and a sign of closed hearts. It starves others of a source of love.

Be obedient to Me and I will bless you. I do not require powerful people. I require prayerful people. I do not ask for hearts burning with zeal. I ask for hearts open to My love.

I can bring about all that I desire. I have all the power necessary to bring My Kingdom in. But how can I usher in My Kingdom if My channels do not carry peace, joy, love, longing for Me? How can I irrigate a parched and dying world if the tributaries of My mighty river of love are silted up and blocked off?

Open your hearts, My people, that I may flow where I will! Do not concern yourself with where that is or who I want to touch. You will feel the power go forth from you when you encounter someone want to love. Be not afraid, but _hear_ what I am saying. If you do not, you too will be lost. You will be lost to a dying world, joining the dust of drought.

You need to hear My voice calling you, entreating you, _moving_ you. Only those who spend time with Me will learn to know My voice. I can use you whether you know My voice or not. It is just that much joy awaits those who spend time in My company and I would like you to have that joy. All of you.

I want to share My presence with you.

Stop coming to the watering hole for your own needs and come, come for the strength to love others. Come to be unblocked, but not for a better life for yourself. Come so that you can be a better, purified channel. I have such love to pour out on My injured and desperate world. If not through you, handpicked and called by name, then who?

Take your eyes off your own problems, dust down the gifts I have given you and unwrap them - for some of you have not even done that. Be willing to be My servant. Humble yourselves and stop playing with Me. Be serious about Me, for we have much to achieve.
I am not a monthly meeting. I am not a rallying cry. I am not a leader of occasional battles.

I AM LORD.

Bow yourselves before Me. Know My majesty. I come in glory to touch your lives, not to be trivialised as some occasional pastime.

112

Do not become casual in your approach to Me, for might and wonder are at My command.

I can stir up the oceans, release mighty winds, peal thunder, flash lightning - and <u>love</u> with all that <u>power</u>. Can you imagine that? Try.

The power is needed. It is being released. Those who will not channel it will be lost to it and will see it rushing past them and their lives. It is both a big and a little thing I ask of you.

I ask obedience to My calling. I ask faith for My words. I give love to all who say 'yes'; love to heal My broken and ailing world.

I love you anyway, so do not fear your hesitation. It will not make Me leave you.

Some will say 'yes' quickly and allow My work to begin in them. Some will be more hesitant as their courage needs to grow. Ask Me for faith. It is My joy to give it. Faith will move mountains and will make you ready to say 'yes' to Me.

I need **commitment**. Commitment to conversion and ongoing change. Start with yourselves. Turn to Me for the conversion <u>you</u> need, for the daily transforming power of God to touch and enliven your lives. Many are dead at the edges, and some hearts too. My Resurrection power will change that, but **I AM THE GIVER**. You must come to Me for <u>daily</u> gifts.

I will change the world through you - if you commit yourselves into my loving, trusting care. You have nothing to fear and much to gain.

My love needs warriors, messengers, servants, listeners, givers, receivers, blessers, people willing to be vulnerable, gentle touchers, happy hearts, willing workers, cheerful givers of money, time, and attention.

113

Somewhere there is a need for you, and you alone, to meet.

If you are unequipped you will not be able to meet that need, no matter how you want to, or how you try.

All the equipment you need is an open-ended heart that receives from Me and gives where I choose and direct.

I will teach you many things if you agree to seek this open-endedness.

You will be surprised at the people I have in mind to touch through   you.

You will be surprised at how little you have to do.

You will be surprised by how much can be achieved.

Often a kind look will bring into being the next step in someone's life.

I will use your eyes, your face, your smile, your touch, to render harmless the evil and hurt in people's lives.

> *Heal My broken world.*
> *Empower My feeble people.*
> *Uplift the discouraged.*
> *Love the neglected.*
> *Start with yourselves.*

Come, to ME, and let Me make of you what I will. "

15 January 1994 9pm

"PRECIOUS TO ME, BELOVED"

"Into an overfilled heart₁ I will pour joy. Into the abundance of yearning I pour prosperity of soul and vision. Into a mind filled with wandering I pour longing for peace. Notice that I pour the longing.

For it is that blessings abound when a believer falters.

Never fear or feel over-run, for I have in My possession many gifts of blessing.

Do not feel at a loss to describe the things that happen. For some things are not for words, they are for safe keeping.

Only be what you are, who you are, and My anointing will flow over you, through you, and then beyond you.

Be certain that you know Me; for I know you.

You are precious to Me, beloved.

Beloved, be of Me. Be patient in my hands. Let Me cradle you, for I have much softness to give you. I will melt the hardness of the years which has encrusted you, making your responses harsh and abrasive. I will soften you, pouring oil on your wounds. The softest of skins will be as coarse cloth compared to the softness I will dress you in. Your mantle will be of finest light and you will spread it around the world.

Only trust in Me and see that I, the Lord your God, mean every word."

Wednesday 23 November 1994

'A FEAST DAY OF MIRACLES'

"This day has come upon you a feast day of miracles. For my blessings are being _poured_ out. Have no fear. I am present in _all_ things. In all your thoughts acknowledge Me. In all your words, own Me. In all your longings, seek Me. In all that you do, find Me.

For I Am all in all to you. I am all that you have ever yearned for, longed for, needed, wanted, desired. I am all that you are. Can you see the mystery in this? How can it be that I am all that you are? Because I abide in you, even as you abide in Me. You will fear no snare, for I have you, safe in the palm of My hand.

I have blessings for you to bestow - to brighten the lives of others who will cross your path. You are a delight to Me and it is _My_ delight to refresh and unburden you.

Release all that you hold, ever, into My waiting arms.

The freedom of this place is a place of meeting, where you and I can be intimate. We will share secrets and longings and I will hear the sweet murmurings of love you speak to Me.

Only seek Me. Never be satisfied with less. Relinquish all cares. Forge ahead in the light of My love and see wonderful things come to pass.

Some you will be part of, some you will observe, but _always_ the _wonder_ will be there. Do not be afraid to watch, to look, to see and you will learn much.

Lean not on your own understanding but always on Me and I will inform your mind of what you need. It really is that easy, My child.

The path of mystery lies ahead of you. Watch it with excitement tinged with fear - of God - for the path leads to Him.

Only let me know how much you love Me,
how much you honour Me, and I will do the rest."

18 February 1995   6.45pm

"YOU WILL FIND ME.."

Q. Where are you, Lord?

A.   *"You will find Me*
In the wind, passing by
Moving the clouds, across the sky;
In the murmur
Of the forest floor
Stirring, stirring,
Stirring once more.
Gently, in the summer breeze,
Lifting and shaking the leaves on the trees.
Breathing on you
As I walk by,
Present in the tiniest sigh
Of your heart. "

Palm Sunday 1995 - 9th April 10 am

I asked:

"WHERE ARE YOU, GOD?"

(In the space between Being and Doing)

"I am in the clouds, in the mountains, in the streams,
In the whisper of the wind passing by,
In the cry of a baby, in the milk of its mother.
I am in the heaven of your heart
*   that passes for understanding*
I am in the new-mown hay.
I am in the dapple of light in the rippling stream.
I am in the longings of your heart
That surface in a dream.
I am in the times gone when life seemed good
I am in the times to come, which seem uncertain and seem
to brood
Despair and darkness.
I am in the looming storm clouds
I am in the angry wind that whips and tears,
I am in the longing of your heart
I am at the centre of your fears.
I am in the highest peak of delight
I am in the place in your mind which lies hidden,
Hoping that none will find it.

I am He who comforts,
Who mourns with the afflicted,
Who sorrows with the bereaved,
Who longs for the companionship of the lonely

119

and downtrodden.
I am He who stands at the gate
Longing and waiting patiently to come in,
Hoping for an invitation to the feast
Of entertainment
Which blinds My people.   1

I am He who stumbles and thirsts after righteousness,
I am He who calls the name out loud
Of all who will hear Me.
I am He who slumbers like a giant.
Tremble when I awaken, for the land will shudder
　　　And mountains will fall.
I will bring fear and trembling into hearts grown cold.
I will bring longing into hearts warm with love.
Know Me by My presence,
　　　By My fruit,
　　　By the Way I come.
You will surely seek Me, all of you,
　　　But many will not find
　　　For they will have left it too late.
　　　Such sad words
*To epitomise the **Coming of the Lord.***
　　　Glorious in majesty
　　　Wonderful in splendour
　　　Mighty in power
　　　As gentle as a Lamb.
Know My words,
Immerse in My knowledge,
　　　In My Being.
Then you will have the answers you seek."

Palm Sunday 1995 9th April 10.40am

"REPENTANCE IN THE SHADOWS"

"Repentance in the shadows
Of your being,
Yielding of the secrets of your heart
Time honoured, time lost,
Time sustained fragments,
Splinters in the soft cloth weave
Of your heart.
See, I remove them.
Feel - they are no longer there.
Touch - the silky softness of new cloth
Unblemished.
Taste, and see, that the Lord
Is sweet
Indeed.

I love you.

Where would I have taken you,
If not on the journey?
To what path would I have called you,
If not this stony one?

Is there a place better,
Safer under foot -
Where sand trickles between your toes

121

And the path is too soft to walk on -
To hold you?
Is it not better to be on solid ground,
To walk a stony path
That bruises your feet
And may cause blood,
Yet holds firm?
I am the Great Physician
Who walks alongside with you.
No cut goes untreated,
No bruise or blemish unnoticed
Or cared for. 1
Believe Me when I say
'I love you'.
Believe Me when I tell you
That you are all in all to ME.
Believe Me when I tell you
I would cross valleys, ravines, mountain tops,
For a glimpse of your love for Me.
Believe Me when I say
'You are Mine'.

I long for you in the quiet of the morning
When dew encrusts the grass.
I long for you in the heat of the day
When cooling shadows offer comfort.
I long for you in the garden at dusk
When twinkling stars appear in the sky.

The dying of the embers of your heart
Are a mighty conflagration to Me

Fanned by the breath of My Spirit.
See, I blow on you
The Mighty Breath of God.
Feel the flames fanned higher
See the blaze of love that
Engulfs you.
Feel the scorch of love
Upon your life. "

"..Or cared for." - means no imperfection matters when the Lord's concern is to tend us.

FATHER, WHAT CAN I ASK YOU FOR?

"You can ask Me for the sun, the moon, the stars,
The wind that passes across the skies,
The dawn of tomorrow,
The last thing at night,
The breath of a baby,
The deepest of sighs
Of contentment.

You can ask Me for the rain of tomorrow,
The sun on the earth,
The grain for the harvest,
The joy of new birth,
The sighs of the lonely,   1
The smile in the heart
Of someone so wounded
They're breaking apart.

You can ask Me for life in abundance
The Ancient of Days,
The Sun of the Morning,
The Light in its rays,
The joy of the suffering,
The pain of the meek,
the lost and the lonely,
The power to seek

Me.
You can ask me for Father,
The joy of My touch,
The sweetest of kisses
As My lips brush your brow.
The certainty of love
The gentleness of touch
The security of My arms,
The warmth of My embrace,
The sweetness of _your_ smile
The sunlight in _your_ life
The joy of _My_ salvation,
Freedom from the strife
Of battle.

You can ask Me for joy in the morning,
A new step at dawn,
A peace in your heart,
A gentleness in your touch,
A smile on your lips,
Soft words in your mouth,
Honey in your heart.

You can ask Me for words in your heart
To guide your footsteps,
Light in your life
To guide your path,
Tenderness in your heart to help others,
Patience in your actions
To stay in My peace. 2
You can ask Me for Me."

"I AM COMING"

"You are to be, for Me, a hand servant, to wait on My pleasure.
I shall anoint your hands with fragrance to soothe My brow.
I shall wash My feet in the tears of your remembering.
You will remember how, in times past, I honoured you and set
you free,
Placing you upon a stone in the midst of a raging river,
Safe, yet abandoned,
Yet not by Me.
For I have loved you with an everlasting love –
A love that yearns for your companionship.
Will you walk the paths of longing with Me, child?
Will you cross the ravines of ravaged lives with Me, honouring the
footsteps of the broken, anointed ones?
Will you step into the furnace of brokenness, even for My name's
sake?
Will I call you again to the path of trouble, where footsteps beckon?
What do you think?
Would I lead you, untrammelled, into less than righteousness?
Would I call you, beckoning your sight on unforgettable horror,
images of war, strewn with bodies of decaying death?
Would I call you beloved?
Would I hear you answer Me, "Yes, Lord"?

For the days of imaginings are long gone
And the day of Atonement is NOW.

Do not think I save you from the fire.
No, rather I baptise you in its flames -
Shriven, refined, purified, beautified.
You are all in all to Me and I will show you how to conquer.
You have come through much.
Tarry no longer in the place of quiet.
The drums are beating and I will lead you on.
March In My footsteps.
Utter My war cry -
>   *of HOPE to people lost*
>   *of JOY to people sorrowing*
>   *of LOVE to those hated and reviled by men.*

For such is the cry of My heart, that My justice abounds.
Too long the words have fallen, lost, dropped down between
the clamour of the world's words.

>   *But now the times will change, MUST change.*

I AM COMING.
I AM LOOKING FOR A PEOPLE IN WAITING.
I AM READY TO ANOINT IN KINGSHIP THE
FOLLOWERS IN MY ARMY.
I AM A CONQUERING KING
I AM A LORD TO DISPEL ALL OTHERS.

Before Me none shall stand
Who do not accept My Hand
In restraint,
In guidance,
In love.
I shall free the yokes of My bound people
Slaying the dragon of success 1

127

Which haunts and ravages My world.
For such as this I did not make the world.
My creation lies, in waiting, to honour My coming.
A waiting creation.
A waiting people,
Draw in your breath and <u>LISTEN</u>.

In the hushed expectancy of a season in waiting,
In drawn in breath of attendant people,
In listening hearts,
The tumult of the mighty, roaring waters will be heard.
Know, then, that **<u>I AM COMING.</u>**
<u>I AM COMING.</u>
<u>I AM COMING.</u>

<u>Share this with the world</u>.
   Notice the unfurling of a leaf
   Waiting to be full, in My sunlight.
   Capture the waiting it shows,
   Learn the waiting it teaches -
   An expectant waiting,
   Waiting for <u>action</u>.
   No passivity or suspended living,
   Fullness of life in the waiting.
As the muscles of a panther poised to spring
Leap, leap into this life of waiting.
Do not be surprised at this moment of unfurling.
   It shall come without your noticing.
   Only be ready.
   I <u>AM</u> <u>COMING</u>. "   2

128

16th October 1996

"A BETROTHAL..BETWEEN MY SON AND MY BRIDE FOR HIM"

"Be at peace, and behold the working of the Lord. A betrothal is taking place between My Son and My Bride for Him. A wedding will follow - sumptuous in its feasting, glorious in its celebrations.

Be assured. Rest assured.

My longing for you is very great.

Your longing for Me is very great.

I will bless your longing and feed you with My presence.

The concerns of your heart concern Me.

You do not need to hear Me say, over and over again, that this is true. Only TRUST Me and see Me work for your longings.

Do you not see that I know, that I care, that I place you before men? Do you not see that I walk the path beside you, yet lead your footsteps?

Do you not see the care and tenderness of My interest?

When will you learn to call Me 'Father'?

When will you learn that the love I have for you is unconditional?

Here, let Me touch your eyes, that they may open and SEE.

Here, let Me touch your lips that they may kiss ME.

Here, let Me touch your heart with fingertips of love, that pain will not indent you.

Only trust Me, child. Only trust Me. Only trust ME, lover of My heart. Light in My life. Only speak to Me, that I might hear the

129

tenderness of your comments.

Only spend time with Me, that I might caress, cradle and love you.

   Know this - you are anointed of Me.

My blessings will flow through you to others.

Nothing is lost or wasted. No moment scorned by Me as too insignificant, or of too little importance. I can use everything - every glance, every word, every sigh, to communicate My love to My world. Notice this - to My world.

   No-one owns it - except Me.

   No-one governs it - except Me.

   No-one knows it - except Me.

No-one idolises it except those who would fornicate with it, in it, and corrupt it.

   My world breathes, by Me.

My people breathe My world and live its pulse. They are its heartbeat.

My people are blessed and anointed by Me and I am raising them up.

   A mighty army is stirring, is on the move, preparing for battle, for WAR.

   The time is NOW.

   Awaken from your slumbers, oh My people.

Your Lord calls you, through the ages, to the end.

I call. I shout "ARISE! ARISE! ARISE!"

   Come forward, come forward!

   Into the plain of battle we will go.

   Take up your arms, bid your farewells.

Do not worry. You will see your loved ones again. Leave them freely, in freedom. Much awaits you - glory, honour and bloodshed.

   But I Am the Lamb, leading you."

"THE LOVE OF THE LORD"

'The love of the Lord' is My Presence on earth.
How else can I be loved?
Open hearts receive Me and release Me.
Such is the mystery of love.
By this means I generate the earth
I create My world
I fulfil and express My longing for My creation.
Know that the abundance of Love is the abundance
of My Spirit.
The one is the other
And the other is the One.
Cause all things to come to Me and
Bathe in this Love.
Then My presence will saturate the earth
And be the earth.
Let all know My words and that I, the Lord,
The King, the glorious Creator,
Live, and breathe, and have My being
In the hearts of men,
Who are My heartbeat.

Never fear, or cease to wonder, at these words.
Pour the longing into My cupped hands
Bathe, then, in the longing
And I will hold you safe.

Abandon yourselves to the longing for Me
And I will do the rest.
Through you all things will be accomplished,
Can be accomplished,
Must be accomplished.
Bathe in the pure water of your longing for Me
And I will do the rest.

"I WAS THERE IN THE SUMMER"

"I was there, in the summer,
When you called My name.
I was there in the winter
When no-one came.
I was there in the clamour of the babbling brook
I was there inside the cover
Of the ancient Book
Of wisdom, love and suffering.

I pointed the way in words of old
Which passed your eyes
And left you cold.
I was there in the tears
Of beggars passing by
Whose eyes were dead
And you asked "Why?"

I met you then in the questions you asked
I led you on 1
Through paths which cast
Their twisting, aimless shadow on you.
You sought me more
You never knew My name or Way.

133

We walked the path of righteousness
Long scorned by clever friends
Your search for Me grew hungry
You bucked the current trends
Of going it alone - and, free,
You sought instead
My face, My fee,
For belonging.

What can I say to you right now?
You've left old ways behind.
We've travelled far along this road
You've found more of your own kind -
Searchers, seekers after truth,
Whose wounds were raw and deep,
Who bled from life's own torment,
And many who lacked the sleep of justice.

With them all you come to Me
You know the truth of old
The message of the Ancient Days
No longer leaves you cold.
You've tried the rest - the drink, the drugs
The sex, the books, the spells
You've left them all, they failed to fill,
Yet still you toil,
You can't be still -
You need My peace.

So ask Me, then, that I may come
A star upon your brow

To soothe the creases of the years
And gently show you how
To love, and serve, and cherish Me -
No price for you to pay -
I'll show you by example
I'll gently show the Way
Of love
And forgiveness
Joy and Peace.

These things to you I freely give
I'll take you to My heart
I'll show you how the grime of old
No longer has a part
In your life.
You will be born again, My friend,
And all things shall be new
You'll know the joy of childhood spent
In freedom, safe from view.

No tongue shall wag, or torture you,
With words that cut like ice
Hurled down into a tender heart,
Because **I've paid** the price
Of Love so strong that none shall break
The seal around your heart
That names you Mine and strengthens you,
You'll always have a part
Of My Kingdom.

My promise now to you is clear
You know what you must do
To place Me first above all else
And then I'll come to you.
I'll make my home inside your heart
Together we'll walk the path
Of wisdom, truth and justice.
These things which touch your heart
Are gifts bestowed by Me at birth
To lead you in My path
Of righteousness.

The healing which you seek, My friend,
Is waiting here for you
To claim in rightful sonship.
I wonder if you knew
How close behind I followed you
When tempters led astray
The greatest one of all is when your thoughts
inside you say
"Who is this Jesus? I don't need Him,
I'm fine on my own."
The freedom felt with no restraint
Is heady stuff indeed
You shut Me out, or seal Me up.
No thought for word or deed
Spent on Me.

I wait, My friend, so patiently
You see, I know the truth
I know the mind's the hardest place

To warm, or light, or soothe.
But you will find your way, My friend,
Your time will be your own.
And I will call you gently and
Wait for you to come home."

"DREAMS SHALL FLICKER"

Into a place of slumber
I will draw you
Where dreams will flicker
Across your eyelids
And show you the wonder of days past.
But this is nothing to the
Wonders of things to come.
Across your eyelids will flicker
Visions of hope
Endorsed by Me
By My power.
And you will see the things to come
With vivid reality.
Not all will be pleasant
But all must happen.
Be not afraid at what I, your Lord,
Will show you.
You will have mountainous visions,
Stormy seas of life,
Battered by gale-force winds of destruction.
The flotsam in the sea
Will be My wounded and ship-wrecked people.
But - I WILL SAVE.
I WILL MAKE WHOLE
I WILL RESTORE.

For these are days of tumultuous outpouring
When visions count for nothing
in the eyes of the unseeing.
But My visionaries _will_ know all.

The path will be hard,
And long hours will be spent in prayer,
For visions bring torment
To the souls of the seers.
Only prayer will ease the burdens.
Only prayer will ease the pain
But this _is_ a _gift_, despite
The longing to achieve peace.
Peace will come
On the wings of a dove
Covenanted by My Father.
The Spirit will be with you
Always.

Trust in Me
And know that you are
Beloved of My heart.
All that is yours will be fruitful.
As I cradle you
So lovingly.
I LOVE YOU."

9th May 1999 1.05pm

SET ASIDE

"Into the <u>stillness</u> of your heart
  I will pour My Spirit.
  Into the <u>stillness</u> of your heart
  I will pour My Peace.
  For where can peace reside
  in turmoil?
  The peace you look for,
  And yearn for,
  Is yours for the asking.
  Only ask
  <u>And</u> receive.
  To receive you must be
  Still.
  You have known this for
  Many years,
  Yet still you dash,
  Your actions a reflection
  Of reaction,
  Not choice.
  Have I not shaped you,
  Called you,
  Informed you,
  Led you,
  Talked to you,
  Of <u>different</u> things?
  Where will you go when the peace runs out?

Will you scrabble,
Like a rat in the dirt,
For a foothold
In the avalanche of life? ₁

If you do not <u>set aside</u> a place, a time,
You will not <u>receive</u>.
<u>I</u> am giving,
Constantly,
Yet you are not receiving.
Make of t<u>his</u> what you will
But recognise the Power
In the words.
Acknowledge it for what IT is
And make your choice."

....

"You are to fill your life with beauty,
This is of My making
That I may encourage,
Strengthen, and
Uplift you,
In all that you do.
Draw on the beauty
As a reservoir,
A source of inspiration
And energy
For you.
Bathe in it,
Delight in it,
For such is My Will,
My blessing,

To gladden your heart.
It is My Will
That your heart is gladdened,
Lightened,
And lifted.

A joyous heart
Floods _nations_
With light.
A joyous heart
Sings My praises.
A joyous heart
Stills the waters of oblivion
In the lost, and aching,
And wounded.
A joyous heart can be still,
Yet exude
My Presence
To a world, broken and wretched.

In the silence of joy
Is light.
In the quietness of joy
A beating heart can be heard.
The beat of the heart,
The breath of the body
- All belong to Me
And _are_ because of Me.
The listener knows the Maker
And lifts the heart _in_ joy.
Joy is _My_ gift

- To a broken people,
An anxious mind,
A calling spirit,
A questing heart.
Display My joy
In the quietness of your heart,
That all may draw to the light,
That joy shines.
Shining is silent,
Shimmering is still,
Yet alive.
My joy is <u>alive</u>.
In hearts that will welcome Me,
My joy <u>lives</u>.
In hearts that will shelter Me,
My joy <u>shines</u>.
Give Me shelter
That I may be in you
And you may be
In Me."

DIARY of the LORD

CONTENTS 2000 - 2006

10.40am 19 December 2000

"A HOLY MARRIAGE AWAITS YOU..
...I AM THE MOMENT"

What do you want of me, God?
> A. *"To keep a steadfast heart and a true spirit."*

And how do I do that?
> *By looking again at the words of your youth.*
> *By seeking Me in all things.*
> *By seeking after Righteousness.*

For only then will you know the meaning of life. You see for answers, but where will you find them ?
Only with Me. Only in Me. Only of Me.
Nowhere else will yield time-honoured truth. No-one else will have the answers, hold the keys to your life, anyone's life.
Everyone needs Me, needs to seek Me.

I will reveal Myself. I will give of My pleasures, My bounty, My blessing.
I will reveal all that is there to be grasped, seen and unseen.
No longer will you walk in darkness, in silence. The dawn approaches, bringing the new day of My coming.
No longer will torment stalk you, or hinder you.
I, I, will speak words, whispers, into your being. You will breathe My words into your soul and springs of water will rise from deep wells of refreshing.

Your tears are the waters of Life - *My life*, in abundance, within you. You have added to their waters over these long days and your sufferings have been real and of account.[1]

> Do not diminish the pain by false measurement. Comparisons serve nothing. Pain is real. Yours has been deep - and deeply moving.[2]

My Spirit cries out to you "Come into the wilderness, My child. Where else can we be alone, together?[3] Where else can we join together and be one? A holy marriage awaits you, beloved of My heart."

Your own marriage is of no concern, no impediment, since I call you to higher union, mystical union, where body and soul are divided; and spirit and soul are united.

> Please Me, by your attendance.
> *Delight* Me with your presence.

Receive the marriage cup of anointing, for the cup is ready to be drunk. Consume the blood of My covenant, the longing of My heart. My heart will then be *your* heart, and you will know anew the calling I am making on your life.

Your tears have opened the way to your heart and I will walk in, now. It has been a long time coming, but I have waited patiently.

Only one day at a time will life be revealed to you. You will only live the moment.

This is My gift to you.

Only the moment, so each is sufficient to itself. Do not look for more - you will not find. Only look for Me, who is the Moment.

I Am the Moment.

Be assured of My love. Be assured of My blessing. Be assured of My peace, beloved of My heart. I love you and I always will. Yours [4] are *safe. Have no fear. Precious as they are to you, who love imperfectly - how much more precious are they to Me?*

I give you glimpses of My heart for them, through your own poor love. Think only, then, of the Love that surrounds them, cherishes them, longs for them.

I am faithful. I am true. I am steadfast.

I am you. 5

You are nothing without Me - and I would be full of you. Pour yourself into Me, so that We may be whole.6

Tenderness awaits you, daughter, lover, confidante, treasure of My heart.

Let me trace, with fingers of love, tenderness into your heart. Veins of pain will disappear as I, the Physician, mend the broken, bruised places.

Your heart is not broken, and will not break - ever - for I am with you, and in you, always.

Turn again, then, as in days of longing, and rest your head on My breast.

Feel my heartbeat and know it is for you.

Rest awhile in My tenderness and be anointed - to love and serve the world, in ways mapped out for you before time began.

I always knew you, knew your faithfulness, despite meanderings. You never rejected Me, even though you walked in clouds of unknowing. 7I was always with you. I never left you. Ever. I told you so the first day you turned to Me. What is true is eternal - without beginning, without end.

This is my love for you - and yours.

Rest a while. Rest a while - and be refreshed, revitalised, restored, renewed, reborn. In Me.

Now - and forever."

149

20 May 2001 11.20am

"I AM THE AUTHOR OF LIFE"

*"I want you to be My amanuensis. I will write the words
for you. Take them in your heart.* 1 *Then you will know that
I, the Lord, am the Author of Life.*
No more will you search fruitlessly in dry, barren places.
The meaning of your life will become clear.
*I will write songs of love, pure joy, in your heart.*2

My mission is to spread **joy** *in a bleak, barren world,
where clouds threaten the skies of My Beloved.*
Sovereignty is <u>Mine</u> *and I will lend My crown to no one -
and n<u>eve</u>r share. Do not be confused by this, or by plausible
claims made by others.*
<u>My</u> <u>Word</u> is t<u>ru</u>e - I alone Am God.
*I Am He who strikes the thunder, cries the rain, smiles the
sun upon <u>My</u> fair earth.*
<u>I AM CREATOR.</u> 3
*In a twinkling of an eye I can destroy all that I have made,
all that is abused and spoiled by greed, famine and
destruction. Arid land is Mine to water. Arid h<u>eart</u>s are <u>Mine</u>
to water, to shower blessings on.*
Despise no one, least of all your self, made in My image.
Turn again to the longings of your heart, to know **My**
longings for you. 4
For I would give you a life so pure, so clear, so devoid of scandal.
I would cause you to shine before many, and ask you for

150

nothing in return, save the love of your heart.

Together we will climb mountains, gaze at waterfalls, marvel at vistas. I will stir, deep in your heart, the responses I need to do My work.

Clear your life of trammels and distractions. Focus on Me. Wait on Me. Set aside your self. Withdraw from the world a while, that I might better bless it through you.

FEAR NOT that these words are of your own making. I naturally speak into your natural needs, but I supernaturally call and endow you with all the strength that you need to see it happen, to see it through.

TRUST ME. I will call on your endeavour. I will bless your work.

I would take you from the false attractions, already like sawdust in your mouth. Let Me Be. Be set free. Spend time with Me. Let us go forward together."

"COME TO THE WEDDING!"

Across all the nations,
Down all the days,
I hear You calling
I seem to hear You say:
"Come to the Wedding!
Prepare for the feast.
Wear only white linen
-And I'll do the rest.

"Come, weary traveller,
Come, fellow poor -
Your trials are behind you
I'll open the door
To a world full of longing
That yearns for your touch.
With arms open wide
Your Father says: "Come -
To a place ready for you
As Bride to My Son.
Your place is assured,
Your kingdom prepared,
My Son needs to rule now
With subjects who've shared
In His passion for loving,
Regardless of foe.

You've overcome hatred
And lies and despair,
You've reached for His glory -
Be ready to wear
The bright crown of righteousness,
Forged in the fire
Of love everlasting
That dispels the mire
Of lives torn asunder,
In a world racked by pain,
Fear and torment, where
There is no gain that
Lasts for a moment
In Heaven's eternal time".

Instead, hear the voice that has
Called all the while,
Leading you home now
"My child, you can smile. 1
The dark days are over,
They've come to an end.
The promise I made you
Comes true as _we_ tend 2
The lives of the needy
From our vantage point
Of Peace, Joy and Love,
As we reach to anoint
The brows lined with fear
Grief, strife and lies.

It's time to come home now
To life in the skies
Of Heaven that waits
For your whispered 'Yes'.
Then hands can reach down,
In a gentle caress,
And lift you to glory
Where Heaven awaits,
Where love knows no ending
And flings wide its gates,
Which seemed closed against you
In life insecure.
So fear not, My Precious,
Your life, now, is here.
With Me
Your Lord
Who loves you"." 3

154

"SPEAK TO MY WORLD"

Speak to My world
Speak to My people
Tell of the things in
The Day of the Lord. 1

Bring it with music
Bring it with singing
Tell everyone -
'It's the time of the Sword.'

The Spirit is moving
He's breathing His fire
His breath is the wind
To fan flames of desire.

So, love Me -
Don't leave Me,
To wander alone -
In times of great trouble
I'm your only home.

You're safe in my Presence
Where all life is precious,
You're safe in My arms
Where all torment takes flight,

155

You're safe to reveal to Me
All kinds of secrets,
You're safe to throw off
The blanket of night.

Night has no terrors
That can ever harm you,
Remember My light is a gift over all,
So come and be blessed
In a place where I cherish
All who will answer,
Respond to My call.

My call is for all ears,
All life in attendance
Waits eagerly for those who answer its claim
On lives left abandoned,
Or broken, or injured,
It's time - really - NOW
To surrender your shame. 2

Your place now is certain
In times rent asunder
By cries of the innocent -
Wild, hurt, and slain -
The fear that you carry
Must leave when I tell it,
And it must take away with it
ALL kinds of pain. 3

156

So fear not, My precious,
Your heart will be cherished
As gently I hold you and carry you home
To a place where I lead you,
To comfort and welcome,
To life everlasting
Because you're My own.

My heart now is for you
So who stands against it?
And what things on earth can begin to tie down
The freed child of God who reaches for loving
When past ties have vanished
And I want you home."

. . . .

Sunday 24 November 2002 c. 8.00 am

"When you speak out what God has done for you,
the blessing will be released." [1]

157

Thank God for healing me three days ago, so that today I could start typing up the messages scribbled on all the scraps of paper. I was praying before starting, when the Lord directed me to Matthew 11.v 15:

"He who has ears to hear, let him hear."
He then gave me the following   1

Tuesday 10th December 2002 12.30 pm

"I AM COMING - LOOK..."

"Go - Tell the nations what I have done, what I am doing.
I will open ears, raise spirits, lift eyes to Heaven, of all who will follow Me.

I Am the Redeemer, the King, Majesty of majesties.
Who will stand against Me?
Who will attribute to others the work of My hands?
Who will come after Me?

For this is the day of the Uprising. The lament over Israel will cease and My Spirit will wage WAR. It is now, the tumult is unleashed. Be on your guard. Be ready. I AM COMING.
You will know this is the hour, the day of My coming, by signs in the heavenlies.

I will arrive in glory.
Look for Me, look for Me, look for Me.

Lift your eyes to heaven and see the majesty unfold.
Look for Me, look for Me, look for Me.

Depend not on your own understanding.
The signs I have put in place before time began are beginning to appear.
How, more clearly, could I show you that I AM who I AM?
Read My Word, soak in it. Lose yourself in Me, that I might set you free to meet Me in the heavenlies.
You know what I am talking about. You know who I AM.
Where else can I take you, to persuade you of My COMING.
Is there a moment to lose, a time of waiting to be ignored, passed over, as of no consequence?

No - the time is NOW.

Sound the trumpet! Call My people!
Tell them, tell them, tell them.
For they must know the truth.
<u>*I AM COMING*</u>.

I need to find them waiting, ready for the Feast.
The Bridegroom is returning and is about to set out.
Be ready, be ready, be ready.
What else must I do, to convince you? Where else must I take you?
What other calamities must befall you, before you acknowledge Me as who I AM?

All glory and honour to Him on the throne; He who rules in majesty, before whom nations and mountains tremble.
*A thunderclap - and **<u>I will be here.</u>***

<u>*Look, watch, wait, listen. I AM COMING"*</u>

160

Friday 13th December 2002 10 pm

"DESIRE ME..REPENT OF LOST WAYS"

"For I would bring you to a place of understanding that touches the hearts and minds of My people. No longer will disdain cover My earth.

No longer will voices raised in rebellion hold sway over My land. My time is coming, is almost here, when I shall hold the kingly sceptre over My subjects.

I will welcome them into My presence and they will kneel before their King.

Make no hasty judgements about this. Prepare, instead, the hearts of My people, to welcome Me, in a time of turmoil.

Despite the affray and affliction, I will hold sway over kingdoms of despots, traitors and valiant strugglers. Times will be hard, but not so hard that My people will break. No reed of Mine shall perish.

Desire Me that I might come and bless.

Desire Me that I Might give Myself to My yearning people.

Desire Me that I might free the captives.

Where will you go, to escape this meeting?
Where can you travel to leave My heart?
Who will take you in, to hide from Me?

Trees and mountains shake in the wind of My coming and I will slay the dragon of discontent. 1

Rebellion plagues my nations. Refusal to accept Me carves denial into stony hearts. But I will bless and water, soften and heal, if My people will turn back to Me.

Call Me. Repent of lost ways2 Oblivion is avoidable. Love can still rule, can still govern, can still minister, can still call - to afflicted hearts, wounded minds, confused emotions, yearning spirits. Try Me - and see.

Remember I am He who can be no other: He who loves, ministers, encourages, holds, cherishes, and gentles into being.
Know Me and love Me - as I do you."

Thursday 23 January 2003 7.50pm

"I AM COMING - SOON..."

"All praise and all thanksgiving be in the hearts and minds of men.

Be anointed of Me and may the desert dry even further, to nothing.
Let the mighty rivers flow, then stop.
Let all who cry out 'Abba, Father' be reconciled, 1 one to another, for the mighty outpouring of the Lord is almost here.

No-one will stand in My Presence who holds anything against his brother.
No-one is worthy of Me, who holds a raised fist against another.
No-one is worthy of Me who hinders the cry of the child, 2 lost and bewildered by war.
No-one is worthy of Me who holds back from helping his brother.
No-one is worthy of Me who holds in his heart the means of salvation and does not share it.

No-one hears My voice who calls in the wilderness of souls long gone, turned away from My Name.
No-one can reach Me who has not known Me.
No-one can be comforted who has turned away.
No-one can reach out and grasp the promises of God who

hurls abuse at another.

No-one can be sure that they are the ones chosen to lead.

No-one can be sure that I, the Lord, have spoken to them unless they seek My face and wait on My voice.

Who knows My voice?

- The anointed ones, the sheep of My pasture; those who come to Me for succour, for strength, for mercy, for tolerance, for pity, for endless love. *These* are the sheep of *My* pasture

Who else dares to call themselves Mine?

Who knows the wrath I store for those who abuse My ways, My wishes, My tiny ones?

Believe Me, the day has long gone when I would overlook the fallen man.

I will rescue and raise up, for it is time. Enough is enough.

I have called, waited, cajoled, enticed, beckoned, encouraged, longed for, dallied for, persisted for - in patience, love and torment - My people, the dear ones of My heart.

Their time is **NOW.** The gates are open and Hell is to be plundered. All days are lost, not spent in My company; and **whole lives** have gone adrift in this way.

But **NO MORE.**

I AM COMING. Look for Me.

It will be **SOON.**"

10.50am Tuesday 8 April 2003

"I AM COMING SOON – I AM TRUTH"

"Peace, peace, My people. You are confused by the advancing of an enemy who brings lies and threats, to whom truth is abhorrent.

Turn again to the voice of your first love. Return me to My rightful place and I will once again speak to you in words you will recognise. My place has been thwarted, usurped by traitors whose treachery is to place other interests above Me. TV dominates; opinions flounder on generated gossip; truth falls between the gaps and is lost to a whole generation.

I will hold accountable those who knew Me, who heard Me – and who squandered Me, treating Me like a disposable, dispensable resource.

I AM who I AM

Nations cower before Me who know the might of My right arm – and they are right to do so. For I have played a part in their lives that is unforgettable – and beyond reason. No thoughts can evict Me from their experience. No words can persuade that I was not there – because they <u>know</u>. And, in <u>knowing</u> Me, they <u>honour</u> Me.
Honour Me, while you still can.
Honour Me, before the days run out.

Honour Me and receive the mighty blessing of freedom in your spirit.

Free spirits praise Me. Free spirits worship Me. Free spirits honour Me.

But a time is coming of enslavement when spirits will cry out for freedom, long ignored and wasted. And rise up and dash freedom on the rocks.

Broken hearts will abound and tears will wash like rivers through lives not spent in My company.

My people, what must I do to warn you?

What must I say to make you hear?

Can you not read the signs of My coming?

Can you not hear the distant drumming of the war that matters?

Look not on false wars. Concern yourself no longer with the frenzy of shouts. Instead be more concerned with the battle each one of you is facing.

Truth must triumph because **I AM TRUTH**.

Concern yourselves with the battle for your souls because this is an eternal conflict. Lose this through ignorance or indifference and you lose everything.

*So, **peace** to you. Peace to you, **My** people. Bathe once again in the waters of purity. Strip yourselves of vanity, possessions and the striving for them. Raise your eyes to the coming Lord, because*

I AM COMING - SOON.

Thursday 8th October 2003   10.00am

"FOOLS FOR THE LORD"

".. Take upon yourself the mantle of obedience. Know that in all things I am directing you. I guide your feet. I am the Path you seek.

Know that I am calling to Myself disciples of faith who will walk Me, talk Me, reveal Me, show Me, demonstrate Me, live for me, die for Me.

The path may not seem to lead to this but, believe Me, it does.

No other feet can walk it except those I anoint. Where, in the world, can I find feet to walk this path? Whose feet may I anoint?

It will be the feet of the wicked, who scorn societies' ways. It will be the feet of the lost, who wander on paths leading nowhere, and not of My making. It will be monstrosities defiled by self-inflicted wounds who will walk My path. 1

For these I CALL.

*They have been rejected by the hardness of heart that My people have allowed to grow within themselves. This callousness is not of Me but is a defence grown by oppression.*2 *My people must melt before I can reach them. My people must, once again, be pliable in My hands, so that fingers of love can retrace their hearts.*3

Where will you go, beloved of My heart, to escape the

167

longing I have for you?

Do not be afraid, or alarmed, that I have known of the callousness. Do I not see the difficulties of this world? Am I not compassionate about how they have affected you?

I would just say that you have made wrong choices - choosing to defend yourself when you should have chosen to abandon yourself to Me. [4]

To lose yourself in Me is fearful, but the fear is not the corrupting kind. That kind is what slips in behind man-made defences, [5] *holding you back from loving those I need loved.*

Only those willing to be Fools for the Lord will reach the lost and aimless. Only those known to be beyond the safety of the churches will understand this call. Only those with fire in their bellies and fear of Me in their hearts will walk this path.

Their voices will penetrate deaf ears.
Their song will calm the beating hearts of the frightened and scared, running for their lives.
Their touch will soothe the world.
Their peace will cover the earth.

So where do you stand in these days? Where will you walk today, tomorrow? I have known your footsteps so far and walked beside you. But we are at a crossroad [6] *and you may choose. Always, you may choose.*

Do not say 'Lord, why?' Just follow, if you want to see My glory."

"A FEAR-FREE WORLD"

"Where would I go? To whom would I run with outstretched hands - if not you?
To whom would I go for comfort - if not you?
Where in the world will <u>*you*</u> *find arms stronger, more comforting, or tender, than Mine?*

> *Will you enfold yourself in My arms?*
> *Will you let My lips brush your brow with the sweetest of kisses?*
> *Will you allow Me, as lover, to touch your soul, anoint your spirit?*
> *Will you welcome Me in to the deepest secret places of your being?*
> *Will you allow Me to love you - to wholeness, forgiveness, grace, compassion, mercy and joy?*

Where else will you find these gifts, these longings, these anointings?

> *There is only one place - and only one Way.*
> *I am both.*
> ***I Am all, in all, to all, for all.***

That means you. I am you. You are Me. We are one in holy matrimony - anointed by My Father, beloved of My mothe,[1] blessed by My Spirit.[2]

> *To you I offer this unity.*
> *What will you do, with this?*

Climb mountains, plunge depths of despair, seek lost?
I hope so.
I have called you to this, before time began.

To these, in darkness, I send My warnings:
   Time is short.
   Life is precious.
   Love is needed.

Fear _must_ flee and release the hearts of massed captives. Fear has no place in _My_ world. ₃ No words of wisdom can echo this because it is a call beyond understanding and the world's knowledge₄
A fear free world has never been known, but it is _My_ will.
Only then will all that _I_ have planted come to fruition.
Only then will the joy that I planned for the world have free flow.
Only then will the laughter of My people anoint My ears like music.
And I would have it this way.
   No longer will fear stalk the minds and hearts of My beloved. I am coming to set them free ₅

Tell them of Me. Tell them of My will in this matter. Tell them to turn to Me, so that I can anoint their ears with Truth, so lies no longer gain entry for fear₆
   Tell them it is _that_ easy.
   Then My love can set them free, _will_ set them free.
   Say this is of Me - for I _love_ them.

   No one else loves like I do.₇ No one else's tender touch can match Mine. No one else's sweet kiss can rouse passion like _I_ can.
   Ask them to place Me before _all_ others - before husbands, wives,

170

brothers, mothers, sisters, fathers, cousins, friends, lovers.

I would be first.
I <u>Am</u> the best, the foremost, the first, the only.

    <u>Desire</u> Me, *that I might bless, with responses to hearts grown cold.* 8
    <u>Desire</u> Me, *that I might anoint the tongues of willing workers to speak My words and release blessings to the multitudes, to the nations.*
    <u>Desire</u> Me, *that I might come again.*

On the wings of desire, much love is released .Love to <u>heal</u> nations, love to <u>anoint</u> nations, love to <u>rescue</u> nations, love to <u>release</u> nations - all from the clutches of evil.
    Evil stalks my world masquerading as fear, enticement, wrong involvement, wrong priorities. People are accustomed to the <u>ugliness</u> of fear and can recognise and turn away - but few see the subtleness of enticement. Here, fear masquerades as tantalising, encouraging just a little step towards the unknown.
That step yields a little knowledge but not all that was anticipated or expected. So just another little step will, surely, show the whole way?
    And so it is My people are duped. Notice I say 'My people'.
I mean <u>all</u> My people. Enticement leads to 'good' things too - 'good' worship, 'good' meetings, 'good' fundraisers, 'good glory.

But does it? Does it lead to <u>Me</u>?

Because there <u>is</u> no 'good' where I am not. And I am in the simplest place and the hardest to access - the <u>heart</u> of the individual.

*So, <u>**wake up**</u>, My people!*

171

Have done with enticement.
Encourage each other in the Way of Truth. I am that Way.
I Am the only Way you need.
Try no other. Seek no other.
There is no other way to My heart.
There is only Me.
*I am all, in all, for all, to all, **all**.*

Try Me and see. Do I not taste good? Am I not the sweetest honey on your lips? Consume Me, with a passion. And I, I will then consume you.
And you will know the answers to all your questions, searchings, longings, meanderings, wandering - as you discover ME, waiting for you.
    Come closer, so I can whisper words of love into your spirits.
Rest awhile in My Presence. Let Me fill you up. Your emptiness is just a waiting for Me, a longing for Me, that has been misunderstood - until now.
        *I have shown you the Way, the Truth. **I AM.***
        Love Me. Love Me. Love Me.
        Before it is too late.
        Love Me.
Anoint Me with kisses. Long for Me - that I might fulfil the calling of My heart for My Bride.

Set aside all that hinders you, all that robs you of time, that leaves no space for Me in busy schedules.
        No schedules can include Me - I do not fit.
        No schedules can hold Me - I am too big.
        No schedules can contain Me -I am too fast,
                too elusive, to pin down.

172

Only your hearts can hold Me - I Am a perfect fit.

Try Me and see for yourselves that <u>I Am who I Am.</u>
  <u>Know </u>Me, finally, for yourselves.

Do not be satisfied with <u>hearing</u> about Me. Engage Me, yearn for Me, long for My touch. Let nothing else satisfy you - only then, will you be ready to be My Bride.
  I Am coming.
  Be ready.

I call down the nations, through the annals of time - let Me know I am welcome.
  Tell Me. Show Me. Call for Me.
  Ease Me into that place of self-containment.
  I will be so gentle
  Find Me here already, when you open up your secret place.
  My heart longs for you.
  Know me - as your Lord, forever and ever."

Wednesday 8 September 2004 3.30pm

"IN THE SPACE BETWEEN NOW AND ETERNITY"

"I Am nearer than your heartbeat,
Hovering over you like wind in the sky
Closer than a hair's breadth
Lost in the space between sighs.
You have looked in many places
Far and between ages
But the place I've languished in.
   waiting for your call,
Is closed to the world.
It is where no one breathes - except Me.
It is where no one moves - except by My Spirit.
It is the space between now and eternity
that waits for your next breath, next step.
You will find me in the rush of air,
The dawn of day
The slumber of rest, true rest -
the stilling of the soul, the mind, the world which holds
you in its thrall.

Cast off the afflictions of the day
that guide your mind, your thoughts, your will,
And listen instead to the beat of My heart.
This will soothe and comfort you, as a mother does a baby.

175

You will hold again the longing of My heart
To see and touch you.
You will know again that My heart beats
For you and yours,
That life can hold no terrors that
 My love cannot measure.
 Your safety is paramount to Me
 And I will lead you to
 A place of refuge,
 Where the world stops.
No longer will you be beholden
To the ways of men.
No longer will you hear the tick of the clock
Counting away your life.
Instead you will hear the reassurance of My heart,
 Beating for you.
 Touch again the love you knew
    - it is still there.
Taste again the sweetness of My smile
    - you still please Me.
 Know again the satisfying
Of the longing of your heart
To touch Me
    - it is still My delight to be real to you."

WHO IS AT MY DOOR?

Q. Who is at my door?
   "The voice of anger, trying to get in."[1]
Q. What must I do, to refuse entry?
   "Be set apart and freed from sin."
Q. Where must I go, to be set apart?
   "Nowhere, my dear - it takes place in your heart.
   Take, first, the time, from a life freely given.
   Then choose the door and step into Heaven.
   Heaven is a place where you and I meet,
   Where life's wailings stop as you place burdens at My feet.
   Look again and see that what I say is true
   As I call from Heaven, waiting to meet you.
   So, do not fear to come, and sit, in My arms
   And I will heal the weight of life's false charms.
   Do not fear to come, My child, and hasten deep within,
   And I will heal the places that have been ravaged by sin.
   Deep furrows of doubt, hard clods of pain,
   All will be soothed and both of us will gain.
   I will gain your heart, Mine to truly love,
   You will gain a life set free by grace from above.
   So do not fear to come, My child,
   And take the life that's yours
   Set free from guilt, remorse and sin,
   Empowered by Me to live a life that's full and free
   And strong and bright,

A life of power, and joy, and might,
That leads to Me;
Across a path that's strewn with wounded, lost,
 and lame,
Who need your face, your smile, your name,
To reach ME, too.
So I'll be Me - and you be you,
Together, alone, we'll take a view
Of earth and all My world could hold
- If only Man would join the fold
    of My sheep.
Gain entry in the heart of sheep without a leader,
Straying to the steep and deadly precipice
Of hearts grown cold and locked in vice.

So what think you now of anger's reach into your life,
To make a breach of confidence in all you say and do?
The plan is foiled, the sheep will tarry,
I need you _now_ - so do not worry.
I'll take your place in life's commitments -
Just hear My voice - and _GO!_"

Tuesday 9th November 2004   1.15pm

"KEY TO MY HEART...SPEND TIME WITH ME..TRUTH"

"I will take you into new places of intercession where the broken hearts will rain down like confetti.

No longer will you seek your own understanding - you will seek Mine. And I have a heart ravaged by the sins of man, torn by their violence to each other and bruised by the spittle when they take My name in swearing.

No longer will you seek the ways of men - for you know the better way. You have the **key to My heart, by spending time with Me** *- and I have given it to you this day, even now.*

You will enter My Heart, safe for all time, and see the wonders as I reveal to you the workings of My Heart. You will not seek comfort for yourself, although you will need it. You will comfort, instead, My *heart - and I will spend the love you give Me in this way :*

I will lay up treasure for hearts abandoned;

I will keep to paths long abandoned souls who would venture forth in the darkness;

I will rescue and uphold the victorious in their hours of battle

And all because you comfort Me.

My Heart belongs to you. You have always known this.

My Heart is your *refuge,* your *strength, and beats for you alone.*

179

You have wandered and tarried for long enough, child.

NOW is the time for change.
So, I am bringing it about.

Where fear stalks the hearts and minds of My beloved, I will wash free with an anointing of Truth so great that many will fall on their faces in awe.
No words will be spoken which will not reverence Me.
No sighs will be made that will not reach Me.
No groans will remain unheard, as I prepare my people for WAR.
The darkness looms but cannot engulf the TRUTH.
Truth is sustainable by faith, a choice underpinned.[1] No things can be said, can be spoken, to bring more life than TRUTH.
Life in abundance is contained in TRUTH.
Truth sets captives free.
Truth anoints willing ears.
Truth sears the mind, making it inviolable.
Truth makes clear the confusions that the world overwhelms with.

Many of these confusions masquerade as CHOICE, but notice I say MASQUERADE for such is the face of evil.
Deceit is nothing to evil; false faces hide the attacking malevolence - but TRUTH discerns all that, sorting good from bad, right from wrong...and sieves the gold from the dross.

Be among My TRUTH givers. Anoint My world with gentleness, for that is true.
Anoint My world with peace - for that, too, is true.
Anoint all comers with the kiss of My embrace – and they

will know for themselves the truth of LOVE.

That is My gift for you today - that you <u>can</u> and <u>will</u> anoint My followers with the kiss of love, in My Name.

    Gain entry, then, into hearts grown cold.

    Gain entry into fearful hearts and drive the enemy out.

Gain entry where the years have chained and shuttered My people into dungeons of their own making - dungeons of avarice, pride, sloth, greed, enmity, disunity, dishonour.

Glorify Me by My presence within you.

Seek Me often for My blessing

*by <u>**SPENDING TIME with ME**</u>*

Then your honour and blessing will know no bounds and I shall be happy within you. Can you imagine that?

    Spread <u>My</u> happiness, through joy, and the world will beat a path to your door.

    Spend time in My presence and I will be able to shape and mould you into a new and different creation - a creation for these days, this time, a blessing to be poured out on nations.

<u>Listen</u> to Me. Heed <u>My</u> word. Lean not on your own understanding - lean on <u>Mine</u>, then all creation will call you blessed, and I will take you to Myself, beloved BRIDE."

Tuesday 1st February 2005

"MY BLOOD IS THICK ENOUGH..WE ARE COMPASSION"

"I know the plans I have for you - plans to prosper and uphold you.

You will never again be counterfeit, lost, or perplexed by My ways.

Your heart has reached a point where I can begin to mould it in My likeness.

Your tongue will speak forth, in whispers, loud proclamations of My glory.

And you will know this glory.

You will see it descend, like a blanket, on the nations who follow Me, who listen to Me, who yearn for Me - starting with Wales.

You seek My face earnestly and I have smiled on you, many times. You have not seen this and nor should you. It is enough that I tell you, so believe. If it were not so, your days would be cold, and long, and dark.

None of these things are true for you and this alone is evidence of My abiding love for you and yours. Life passes so quickly that it leaves you breathless - and so it should - for the days are hurtling towards the abyss1 - from where all hope comes.

The abyss is not a place of blackness -it is a place of bleakness where hope lies untouched..

...untouched because unrequited. Who has need of hope when self proclaims all help? 2

This age is insidious, invidious, unsealed and open to the elements of greed and excess.
In search of something of lasting worth man seeks impact –
a scurrilous counterfeit, and one you have sought in place of Me. 3
When you have searched for My face, you have looked for impact, as sensation has meant real to you.
*No longer walk this path. Walk, instead, the Path of Unknowing*4
Be assured of My Presence there.
*Rest content that Unknowing is more real than a thousand fold impact. It is a place of **trust**, of knowledge gleaned from **My** fields - not the fields of man's knowledge of Me* 5 *These are brightly decorated with baubles*6 *to catch the light –*
*but I **AM** the LIGHT.*
I am what they, and you, seek.
No one comes to Me unless the Father says so.
No one glimpses the Father except through Me.
*The haze of blood which clouds My Father's vision is **Mine**. Through it He sees only purified perfection - a focus I earned. You did not. No one has.*7 *Nothing can match **My** sacrifice. No personal loss or grief can touch My Father's.*
*But **We are** compassion.*8

All that you seek, for you and yours, is yours through My blood. My blood is thick enough to cover all sins - it will not fall away. It will coat each and every sin and corrode the dark roots, eating like acid into rust, leaving purified metal beneath - metal that is pure and clean and strong, ready for the Refiner's fire.

183

You are safe from all that ails you.
Nothing can withstand the power of My love over you - and you are deluged by My love, a constant waterfall upon your head. **NOTHING**, *and* **NO ONE**, *can alter that.*

Be of good faith - TRUST ME and leave all things to Me.
I alone will guide your paths and secure your footholds. My Word is a lamp unto your feet. Look and see that I mean it. I love you."

Thursday 10th February 2005   9.30 am

"BUT I FASTED FOR YOU...LISTEN"

"But I fasted for you.₁ In the Garden of Gethsemane I fasted My life, that you should have yours, in abundance.

I fasted My right to live, so that <u>you</u> could.

So make of it what you will. This is My gift to you.

Know that the end of times is fast approaching. Do not deviate from the path laid before you. Your footsteps are very necessary and will forge a path for others.

*Do not look to left or right for the moment is <u>now</u> when I will take you to Myself in an embrace so loving, so powerful that <u>**all**</u> else pales beside it.*

You will not look for another, or other, as together we make the love that encompasses the world - as was My desire from the beginning.

Together we will walk paths scorned by others. Together we will visit remote places, barren and devoid of life, of breath, dust-ridden and debris-filled.

You will not know of these things, when they will occur. You will simply be there and look for Me, sometimes in panic, but fear not.

*<u>**I WILL be there.**</u>*

*I will be waiting for your look, waiting for your search for Me, waiting to respond as you reach the place <u>**I**</u> have carved out for you.*

185

This has been planned for all time, for the moments lie ahead when I will pour forth My Spirit on you and on those who will **LISTEN.** Hearing is not enough.

Listening requires response - and that is what I am seeking. Heartfelt responses warm *My* heart and release all that it is holding in blessing for My world of wounded people.

So, **LISTEN** and **RESPOND.**

I will guide the path of response. Do not look for detail ... leave that to Me, for I alone know perfectly how to perfectly meet the needs. Be My mouth piece, My agent for change, life-giving change.

Release the captives.
Abandon the mighty.
Loose the fetters that chain My people.
Show them the 'Way to My Heart'. ₂
I will show you. You show others.
Know I am telling you this. Relax and listen; do not hear. LISTEN.

Then I will bless all that you do and say in My name. I will pour down blessings and power that will anoint your heart, your mind, your actions.

You will reach forth your hand and **SLAY THE DRAGON** of contempt and false righteousness that dogs My followers.₃

Lead them to purity. Be purified again yourself.

Let me show you how.

186

The path of nurture lies before you. Step on it willingly. Be fed the bread of praise which will be sour in your stomach.4 Turn to Me for soothing. Let Me know you know the difference between the praise of man and the glory of God.

Bask in My glory in secluded places - do not seek it for yourself.

I do not need to satisfy your whim to see, because I Myself place within you seeds of glory to share and plant and water with your tears.

Bless others. Seek only to bless others and all else will come to you.

Trust me for all things, all ways, all paths, all answers, all directions.

Know Me - as I know you - indivisibly.

Pray, and bless Me too - such is your (everyone's) gift, that I might be sweetly succoured and strengthened for what lies ahead.

Know Me as your Lord, your Comforter, your Bridegroom, that I might softly kiss your eyes, closed in prayer and expectation of My coming.

Know that I have blessed you, am blessing you, in all ways, all days of your life.

Bless Me, that I might praise your name to the Father.

I love you, precious of My heart."

Friday 11 February 20005   1.30am

Following on from yesterday, I asked the Lord about the 'Way to My Heart'.

'WAY TO MY HEART'

Q. What is the 'Way to My Heart', Lord?

"It is a way of journeying, of reaching beyond the present to the ever-present, from the now to the eternal, which holds the now."

Q. And how do I find the 'Way', Lord?

"By spending time in My presence and by letting Me warm your heart. My fingers will re-write the responses of your heart - putting love where fear ruled; placing gentleness where tyranny 1 broadcast self-righteousness.
Where in the world will you find such love?
- Hanging on a tree."

188

Tuesday 8 March 2005

"UNITY / MY ALTAR OF LOVE"

"In the days of outpouring, My Spirit will descend like a blanket. No longer will people search the byways for a sign. I will be what they seek. I have always been, but they have sought power and signs, when they should have looked for ME.

I Am in all things, in all places - in the faces of the young, the old, the rejected, the lost, the gnarled, the tortured, the wizen, the foolish, the marginalised, the crooked, the funny, the forlorn, the weary, the foot-sore, the victim, the perpetrator, the left, the abandoned, the found, the silent, the hungry, the lost, the aided, the abetted, the disabled, the enabled, the worldly-wise and the innocent.

Where, when all this is available, is there anywhere else to look?

To whom would I turn, if I were looking for you?

Where would I find you?

The only place is where you are and I would start there.

So, be of good cheer, My people. How can you miss Me? How can you not encounter Me?

Have done with ways of impact and impression.

Know that the face I have for you is one that is wistful, hoping, enquiring, loving, smiling My joy into your eyes.

The encounter we can have yields satisfaction beyond words.

No action on your part, to these My little ones,1 can yield

189

anything but heart touches. _You_ give - _they_ touch your
heart.₂ This way your heart comes alive and courses with **My**
Love.

I would have it this way, for hearts _must_ beat with **My**
Love - or else, in this world, they beat with fear, for war.

Do not let the times distract you from My purpose.

I would have **LOVE** enfold the world.

I already made this possible in My beloved Son.   To whom
would you go, if not to Him? To whom would you pour out
your sorrows, your lies,₃ your hopes, your endeavours, if not
to Him?

 He hears _all_ things _well._ He _makes_ all things _well._

He changes, in the twinkling of an eye, hearts grown leaden.

He brings joy and rejoicing, to enjoy and be enjoyed.

You _are_ supposed to _enjoy_ life.

You _are_ supposed to be _enjoyed_ by those who know you.

Such is the blessing I command on those who dwell in unity.

 It is My will that UNITY is a word lifted from the table of politics;
and placed where it belongs - on _My_ altar of LOVE.

Sacrificial love builds altars.

Giving of self _is_ sacrifice.

Give of yourselves, one to another, in blessing and love.

Command the words of peace and _bring_ them into conversations.
Do not let an opportunity slip by, a conversation to be without_
peace.
Make of this what you will, knowing that _My_ will is to bring peace
between brothers.

Brothers-in-arms must find another way.

Lay down your weapons of destruction, fine-honed in the
furnaces of hatred and despair.

190

I bring another way - the Way of Peace and Joy and LOVE –
words that count for nothing in the rush of anger.
But seek Me. Seek Me in <u>all</u> things, and *I* will dissipate the anger.
<u>Give</u> it to ME. <u>Release</u> it to Me. <u>Trust</u> Me to make of it what *I* will -
and I will use the fiery energy, transforming it into the POWER to
love.4

Let Me. Let Me change you. Let Me know that your heart's
desire is for peace and *I, I* <u>alone,</u> will accomplish in your spirits
what your hearts yearn for.

Thus accomplished, your hearts will <u>yearn</u> for peace and a
sickness of war will result.

Open your eyes and see Me in the places and faces of the
dispossessed.
Know that the gamble for life is here.
Miss this opportunity and there may not be another.
I warn you all. My day is fast approaching - and I <u>will</u> smite My
enemies.
Do not be daunted, or let fear trouble your souls or cloud your eyes.
I Am <u>greater</u> than all fear - and My power lies in **<u>LOVE</u>**.
Avail yourselves of <u>this</u> power.
LOVE and **<u>be</u>** loved - by Me; through Me.
Know that in all things *I* know and love you.
Be assured of My love.
Revel in it.
Be joyous in it.

<u>ENJOY</u> Me - as I do you, Beloved of My Heart,
and <u>you</u> <u>will</u> see My glory, as it falls."

191

Monday 16 MAY 2005 11.05am

"LOVE...POURED OUT IN DARKNESS
..SPEAK FROM THE HEART"

"It is now time to open My hand and release, to the world, the final offering for their salvation.

No longer will the world wait for direction because the ultimate direction is here in My words.

It is not My will to lose even one of My little ones. I wish to pour balm on their wounds, bind up their broken hearts, pour love into these cracked vessels, because they know - better than anyone - how much that love is needed by their fellow travellers; and they can give it while they are still close to them, before their light becomes too brilliant and dazzling to those who walk in darkness. 1

<u>Love can be poured out in darkness</u>.

The greatest love was poured out in the deepest darkness, on the Cross.

Remember that.

Love does not need eyes. It needs a heart. So it is alright to walk in <u>blind</u> faith, unseeing and unknowing, sharing the discomfort of the walking dead. Because love <u>conquers</u> all.

As kittens cannot see their mother, yet receive her tender ministrations in fullness of trust and expectation, so love can gain entry into those whose blindness is caused by the darkness they inhabit.

As a kitten recognises the touch of their mother, so <u>all</u> <u>hearts</u> recognise the touch of <u>My</u> <u>love</u> because <u>I</u> have made it so.

193

So go to the place* I have appointed for you.
Receive the blessing of the anointing.
Know that I AM your GOD.
Worship Me in fullness of TRUTH. " 2

* Where is the place, Lord?
"In My heart. You will find Me there with the cup of anointing."

How do I get there, Lord?
"Pray, pray, pray - until prayer becomes a joy. That joy is the door I open, in welcome. Go through the joy to the place of anointing; and you will know <u>all</u> that I have for you."

Thursday 16 June 2005 10.00am

"I AM THE KEY...FOR THE UNFORGIVEN"

"The cup of anointing will be bitter. It will trickle down your throat and put fire in your belly.

This is the anointing that will follow - that My love is poured out over the lost, the ailing; the weak; the sinner; the unforgiven 1 - for I would touch their hearts, too, broken by remorse that will not be accepted.

Tell them that I will heal them of the tortures they are going through. Tell them that I will restore to them the life they have lost in atoning. Tell them I have seen their struggles, their heart-felt wish to make amends - and I accept their efforts.

I accept their remorse. I find them acceptable. I love them. They can safely discard all others and release themselves from the yoke that binds them to the unforgiving others. I would not have them bound any longer.

Tell them to turn to Me, so that I can receive their efforts, their struggles.

I am a gracious God and I receive all that ails them, all that troubles their spirit. Tell them to start with their sin - that which caused heart-ache and offence.

Not only will I receive this from them, as well as the atonement, I will then set free those sinned against and hurt by their transgressions.

If the sinner turns to Me, <u>I will heal the sinned against</u> ₂
It requires this. Tell them. Tell them to <u>trust</u> Me, to <u>do</u> it, and to <u>watch Me</u> work. I will accomplish, in a twinkling of an eye, all that has been held in deadlock. I have the key to unlock.

    I <u>AM</u> the <u>KEY</u> *to unlock hatred, bitterness, unforgiveness, drought in the soul, pain in the mind, twists in the body.*
    TRY ME and SEE that I tell the Truth. *I <u>AM</u> the* **TRUTH, the WAY, the LIFE** *that eludes them.*
    They have tried with all of their being. Now try with Mine. Because <u>I</u> <u>AM</u>.

I render the past nothing. No giants to loom over in the darkness of memory. No scalding touches of shame to desecrate or spoil a new beginning.
The freshness of new life is what <u>I</u> offer. No human effort can bring this about. But <u>I</u> can.

<u>I CAN</u>.

Watch Me. Try Me. See for yourselves that I <u>speak</u> the **TRUTH.**
I <u>speak</u> the **TRUTH** *into* **BEING.** *Try Me and see.*

    Taste Me - Am I not sweet? Do I not replace the bitterness of the years past with lightness and sweetness? These are yours for the asking. It is My joy and My delight to give.
If you wish to receive, TURN *to Me - and let Me kiss away your longing and your pain.*
    My kiss is gentle and tender, with a passion that lights up your heart, setting it on fire for **ME**. *I would be* **<u>first</u>** *in your heart, before pain, before anguish, before hatred, before lies, before scorn, before enmity, before cultural divides.*

196

I can dwell in these dark places and bring light to illuminate the falseness of these beliefs that have choked your heart. These idols of satisfaction 3 have not yielded what you desired. They did not bring satisfaction ......they brought dis-ease, malfunction, disorder, worry and chaos your lives.

    I would restore what these locusts have stripped from you. Will you let Me? Will you allow Me to enter in and bring _new life_? Would you let Me kiss you with the tenderest of kisses and soothe away the pain that has knotted your stomach, blinded your mind so that you could not see the Way forward?

    I will touch the willing, the hopeful, the desperate, the anguished the lost, the seeking, the anointed, the pain-ridden, the bound, the lost - and **SET THEM FREE**, if _only_ they will turn to Me. _Tell them._ _Tell them_ to turn to Me and **_ENJOY ME_** for themselves.
        I do not offer second-hand words.
        I do not offer second-hand experiences.
        I offer **MY SELF** - to be **_ENJOYED_**.

    I offer Joy to ailing hearts. I offer JOY, clear and bright, to confused minds.
I offer clarity of vision to those blinded by loneliness and pain. **_I_** see _them_ clearly and they are _lovely_ to ME.
Tell them of their _loveliness_. They will not know the word is for them. Tell them. _Reassure_ them. _Convince_ them that **I MEAN** it.
It is a word _for_ _them_.
It fits like no other because **I** **_see_** beyond the blackness of their souls, beyond the bleakness in their lives - and **I** **_will_** **RESTORE**, if _they_ will _allow_ Me.
        I do not press in.
        I will _not_ pressure them.

I will wait, patiently, for their answer, hoping for their response.
This is a love call, a call of love to unloved souls....

Let spirits soar when they hear My voice, the voice of the MASTER.

I will defeat all enemies.

I will vanquish the hordes that play havoc in lives that belong to Me 4

*I will overcome the enemies of those who will turn to Me, for NO-ONE raises a hand against those who are **MINE** and it go unnoticed by Me.*

I will deal with enemy action. I will rescue those oppressed by forces beyond their control or influence.

WATCH ME KEEP MY WORD.

*The **BATTLE** is **MINE** and **ALREADY WON,** but the Enemy does not know this.*

Be on My winning side.

***DEFECT** from his control. Weaken his army.*

***JOIN ME** and together we will dance in victory over evil in this, My, world.*

My creation was made in love, of beauty, for joy - and I would restore what the Enemy has corrupted. He enjoys desecration and has much to answer for. He will answer - and be accountable for all lives spoiled, robbed and tainted by his touch. He will be overcome. He has no choice.

*I have it **ALL** - because it is all Mine.*

***EVERYTHING** is Mine.*

***EVERYONE** is Mine.*

Some choose against Me.

*But this is a **FINAL** call to make a choice, again I equip you to make it.*

198

CALL on Me.
Make a choice for LOVE.
Take a stand against hatred and fear. Be brave. Take the courage I give you.
Choose Me. Choose Life. Choose Light.
Choose JESUS - name above all names.
Name above hatred and despair.
Name of blessing over all.
Name poured out for you.

Do you know Me?
Do you want to?"

Saturday 9 JULY 2005   11.30am

"I AM THE DEPTH, THE BLESSING, THE COMPASSION"

"Come again to the quiet place - to the place I have prepared for you. Do not look to see if the world is there. In this way of looking, much is lost. Much is given to those whose voice I long to hear - in that quiet place.

The place of calling holds all I have to give.

It holds ME.

To whom would I offer this, if not you?

To whom would hands of love extend if not to those needing?

That means all. All for all.1 Everyone needs love, needs Me.

Few know the depth of the longing I have for you all.

Some feel the tug in their heart.

All need their hearts rekindled.

Desire is weak for Me in the nations. Compassion is one part of My desire for them. Where compassion is, I rule in hearts.

Even hearts who do not know Me, yet.

My finger of love writes compassion in responses and I have placed before you times for compassion.

Let it flow, washing hearts clean of grime and impurities.

Let compassion be the dividing line and the sides for good and evil will become clear.

You will know which side you are on when you see where

you are standing.

Recognise - then act. Do not let the location be the beginning and the end.

*If you stand, with compassion, do not be satisfied. Look for more; look for love; look for **ME** - because I am at the end of the line that starts at your feet of compassion. Do not say "I only did what anyone would do" because that is not true. You did what_I would do - and what you did is of ME.*

Look around you. Plenty of others would not have done what you did, pleading distaste, dislike, disgust - their hearts were willing but their flesh was weak.

And others would contain their actions, allowing no impulse to deter or distract them from choices made in establishment. 2

> *Establishment3 selects according to ideas and builds a castle of containment. 4*

> *It feels secure, strong, able to repel the enemy and keep him outside the gate.*

> *But this is a castle of fear, 5 keeping in the beating hearts of compassion and keeping out the bleeding and broken, hungry and lost.*

Fear is a demolition, not an establishment. The castle is a stronghold, but not of My making. Then all that can reside in it is that which contains, which limits, which oppresses, which curtails freedom. And the builder, king of the castle, is the prisoner; and the ruler is the ENEMY.

Think on this. Think at these times and choose COMPASSION. It will lead to Me.

Even those whose establishment echoes with war and cries of innocent victims can make a different choice. Cross the line. Defect from the Enemy. Come to ME.

I will make whole partial thinking, partitioned minds, brutalised beings.

All flesh will know Me, will recognise Me, will belong to Me, for they are Mine and beautiful in their brutalising. 6

I see the depths of minds made whole. I see the blessing of minds renewed. I see the longing of hearts torn with compassion.

I _AM_ the depth, the blessing, the COMPASSION.

So turn to Me for anointing that I might pour balm and blessing into wounded minds.

Balm and blessing, blood and joy - these are Mine to give. Solace is found in these gifts. _Blood_ of My _Son_. _Joy_ of My _Heart_ - what can stand against them? Blood brings healing; joy gives strength. What more is required?

Gentleness of spirit is a grace bestowed by Me on healed minds. Where rawness of emotion tears the mind apart, _I_ will touch and make whole. Where scars of old wounds pulse with pain

- _I_ will soothe with peace.

Where songs of righteousness 7 *strain the ears, _I_ will bring music of contentment, to soothe the stirrings of the incitement. I will bring* **PEACE.** *I will bring* **CONTENTMENT.**

I will slay disillusionment which saps the energy of people meant for **LIFE.**

My heart is full to bursting with **LOVE.** *Let Me pour it out. Let Me empty Myself into you, then pour Me out over others. Where can I go, if not to you? Whom can I ask, if not you? _Must_ I be everywhere and do everything Myself? Or can I trust that the cry of My Heart will be heard, will be responded to?*

Please, My people, hear Me."

Monday 15 August 2005 9.20 am

"SACRIFICE"

"Hearts that break with sacrifice ₁ gild My crown. Lilies were never fairer. Poured out upon My aching world, sacrifice commands a blessing. Notice I say "poured out".

Held in, or kept to oneself, sacrifice eats at the heart.. destroying the path, laid out ahead, of light and goodness.

In the midst of the sacrifice it feels dark, but this is the place of the closed heart.

Once open to sacrifice, the heart is illumined by joy. So sacrifice is to be <u>embraced</u>, <u>enjoyed</u>, welcomed for its blessing. Blessing is not always pretty or comfortable, but the searing of the blessing cauterises the heart that would lose its life blood to the hardening of selfishness. Once sealed, <u>life</u> flows.

It is a hard place to be and not one that many enter willingly.   Few know the surrender of the heart or the blessing of sacrifice.   What are life's losses, but small invitations to take another step on the path of Life, to LIFE in abundance. And even then, the CROSS is at the end, beckoning on.

Hearts quail at the sight, at the thought of ultimate sacrifice.

But you knew this, daughter, when I spoke to you many years ago.   And you said 'Yes' to unknown sacrifice. And this is some of that unknown.

You do not need to worry.   All is at hand. Your sacrifice was graceless ₂ to teach you the way of hardness. Notice I say "hardness" not harshness. The place of hardness refines you and allows your suffering to be seen by others, not concealed for their temporary comfort. It is a place of reckoning - and reckoning for all.₃

Your suffering has been great and will continue to be great, whenever I choose, because My purposes have merit, accomplishing beyond the seen. You do not yet know about these things but I will one day show you. Meanwhile ponder on this.

The death of My Son on the cross accomplished beyond the seen. Now do you understand? He did not cry for Himself. He travailed for others. He suffered the path of acceptance *in My arms.* You can do the same.

I offer My arms to you, secure, safe, comforted, understood, nourished for the journey ahead - what more could you ask, or desire?

Do not fear to ask, or fear to walk the path. It is laid out for you and every stone crafted and placed by <u>My</u> hand. You know that every bruise to your feet concerns Me and brings My loving touch, so look how close I am to you, how <u>**I**</u> minister to you, how I Am the great Physician.

Do you know a better place than the place of constant tending?

Do you know a more comforting encounter than the touch of My hand?

…..Waiting on someone in love is not the simplistic, superficial place of sweetness. It is the place of **<u>longing</u>**. Understand this, daughter. <u>Know</u> that this is what you agreed to. So much of your agreement has been in blind faith.

Now I will open your eyes to see the cost.

I did this, this time .*That* is why the pain has been so great. You could *see* the path - and still chose it, for the greater love of .... He will *know* this, too, *now* - *because* you suffered for the gift. He will wonder and I will touch his heart and release .....

I promised you a h*ar*d path, daughter. Now learn the *joy* of the hard place, the d*urability* of the hard place, the *stability* of the hard place. You will encounter *love* in abundance, in the hard place - for where else can power like this be held? Where else provides the strength underfoot to hold the power of love? I am talking about the love that blows holes in people's minds; the love that casts out darkness and the minions of darkness; the love that encounters fools, lost in their own self-importance, *contained in their castles* 4 and is strong enough to call them out.

Lazarus, in his death, responded to that love. If this love can call someone to *life*, imagine the *power*.

It needs a *strong* resting place, hard and solid underfoot, that will not yield and waste it. It **cannot** be **contained**; it must **not** be contained; it is a moving, living force that hovers over the waters of life, bringing refreshment, hope, abundance into parched lives.

My vessels, My resting places, must be refined and pure, capable of holding with no weak spots penetrable to the enemy.

You have had weak spots and I have accomplished the strengthening.

Watch and see, as the days unfold, that the purpose of this

205

suffering is to draw .... If you had known, you would not have walked this path. Your compassion for him has avoided this place in the past and limited you to the path of compassion.

But I call you to a higher, deeper path of LOVE. It is not a place of <u>understanding</u>, but of <u>revelation</u>. Revelation <u>brings</u> understanding, so you will not be confused or blind any longer.

I know the longings of your heart, daughter. I understand the need to know, but I have tamed this in you. Your spirit is becoming docile, ready to respond to the Master's voice.

Before your docility was not real. It was passivity that 'felt' docile. See the difference? Distinguish the difference. <u>DISCERN</u> the real from the s<u>ubstitute</u>. Do not settle for the su<u>bstitute</u> any longer.

<u>This</u> place of Truth requires courage - courage of expression, regardless of cost to you, or others. Relinquish the guardianship of others' feelings. I did not give it to you. It has been a protective instinct, forged in your own image, brought from <u>your</u> own place of pain. It is a living out of kindness, but a kindness b<u>olted</u> on to pain, not a kindness born of love. It is time now to relinquish <u>all</u> old ways. You can, finally, hear Me and your spirit is obedient and malleable.

The stripping has been vital for <u>your</u> well-being. So many layers of defences - and you thought they belonged to others. In fact, it has been <u>your</u> defences that have been stripped away.

I have cherished ... and held him and his suffering has been to tenderise <u>your</u> heart, daughter. And you have sat in judgement instead. Now, perhaps, the time has come to change all this.

*Your protection and control is no longer needed. Your judgement is redundant and just forges chains of repression. You can receive these words without condemnation, but you do need **abandonment** - to My word.*

*You have not asked Me for this, preferring haphazard dipping. Now I call, I **COMMAND** you to **BATHE** in **My WORD**.*

Not to do so is pure folly.

*The times are hard, harsh, unforgiving, relentless in violence and hatred. Only LOVE stands against this. Only LOVE survives these times. If you do not **BATHE**, you will not LOVE. **I need LOVERS**, to save My world, to be in My world, to bring light into darkness. I called you a wand - I want you to be a BEACON. I want more of you. I want to make more of you.*

The words forming in your heart will be informed by My WORD. You need this in-forming. Look on this. Dwell on this. Meditate on this. Feed on this. Digest this and be nourished by the in-forming.

Your words are IMPORTANT. Do not worry about time or place. These matters are in hand - in My hand. So what is it to you, otherwise.

> *I can wake you up, put you to sleep, revive you, revitalise you, protect you from noise, distraction and false values. I can place you on a pedestal, trample you underfoot, place you in the ground and call you from the tomb of self-interest, self-containment, self-owning and personal responsibility and self-directing control. You are nothing in My hands and everything I want. You are precious, beloved, of more value than the universe. I would walk deserts, cross mountains, surge through oceans to be with you. Notice **I** come **to you**.*

207

Why would I do that, if not to tell you 'I love you'. I come **to** you. Wait, then, for your beloved.

Remember the place of longing. It is our meeting place. I have kept appointments with you before. Wait for the Bridegroom who longs for the sweetness of your kisses. They are wine to Me. Did you not know that, precious of My heart? Dwell on these words. They are for **you**. They speak of My passion for you. All that you have longed for is yours, already yours.

RECEIVE. BELIEVE. THANK. PRAISE.

Be filled with **JOY** - it is your bridal head-dress and will flash with brilliance, sending shafts of light into dark places, lighting up the shadows for people who struggle to see; and bringing beauty into forlorn hearts,

Trust Me. Taste Me. Am I not sweet and lovely?

Be enthroned with Me. Rule with Me. Govern My world in Love, with Love, by Love.

Recreate the tenderness long gone in hearts that are cold and miserable.

Drip the honey of My Presence into the waiting, starving lips, opened in wailing loss. Soothe the brows hardened by loss and fear until the furrows subside. Bring comfort to the world, in My Name.

What loss, then, is yours, that can be counted worthy of Me?

Is there a competition? Is loss measured by judgement?

No, it is measured by the tenderness of heart that is left. Loss, accepted in sacrifice, yields a harvest of tenderness. Loss, scrutinised by understanding, evaluated for merit, dries out the soul, making it arid desert where I would put love to grow.

Your job has always been to water My ground. I plant - you water. Your tears, your words, do this.

Your tears of suffering, your shared words of comfort, water in different ways - but they are the waters of salvation for arid places. Receive this. Dwell on 'SALVATION' and apply what you learn in this way. You will not know the way to turn, the direction you must travel in, but you do not, now, need to know - anything.

Is this not a great release I have given you? Can you measure the distance you have travelled? Do you remember the intensity of your need to know? It is only a heartbeat away - but it is the beat of My heart. Consider this. One of My heartbeats carries you this far, takes this time.

Do you want more? Will you sit in My arms and lean your face against My heart? Will you listen to its beat, learn its rhythm, see what makes it pace? Will you go into My world and speak of My heart? Will you let me give you My heart? Will you suffer as My heart suffers? Will you LOVE, as MY heart loves?"

....

"Then be prepared for the battle. It is in the Darkness, of the darkness, and many prisoners need rescuing. Daringly snatch those I long for, languishing in prisons of their own making, of their own containment.

Speak words of command and the prison doors will open. Vanquish guards with PURITY. They will NOT stand against you. Many will simply flee at your glance. Others will resist and even attack you, but you will always escape with the rescued ones and bring them to the waiting safety, succour and restoration of the LIFE and LIGHT that has always been there for them. Open their eyes with the gentlest of touches, the lightest of kisses, the most sensitive of words.

  Watch your life grow and change.
  Watch the path unfold ahead of you.
Know that in all things I count you blessed, I call you 'Beloved'. For you are dear to Me and <u>together</u> we will conquer the foes ahead.
  Have no fear.
  *Know that in all things **I <u>AM</u> <u>WITH</u>** you.*

*Your book is an accomplishment waiting to happen. It is already done. It is already written. **<u>Ask</u>** Me for the words. I am ready to give them to you now. It is not that <u>you</u> have not been ready. It is that <u>I</u> have not been willing to give them to you until now, until the place of suffering was established.*

Yesterday did that. You heard in that place the lying voice of temptation[5] and recognised it for what it is. It <u>is</u> the same voice that self-harmers[6] hear that leads them to self-destruction. You defeated that by <u>simple</u> expression of <u>simple truth,</u> by denying the 'truth' of the <u>feeling</u>. It is an emotional minefield that Satan plants. Defuse the mines. This is the landscape I have in mind for you.
  Bomb disposal experts communicate with their superiors.

  *<u>I</u> am **<u>Yours</u>**. <u>Stay in touch at all times</u>.*
  Know Me by the beat of My heart. It is yours."

"MORE LOVERS...THE QUEUE OF LIFE
...ARMOURER'S QUEUE"

"Without Me, you can do nothing.
With Me, you can travel universes, climb mountains, fly over unparalleled vistas, known only to your imagination and the secret places of your heart.

Pouring into the heart of love, I come. Blessings abound as Love enters, finding its course. No path will go untravelled, no footstep unlit. The deepest, darkest corners of the journey will be illumined by the flame of Love.

Love passes through, bringing light and power, sweeping in an instant through the cut-off places in the labyrinth of lost life.

I will reconnect.
I will restore.

I will ensure that dark places, festering with foetid remains, are lit by the sunlight of My love.

I will heal. I will restore. I will encourage. I will lighten the load by carrying it for you. You will no longer carry the burden but be My hands to minister these things of recompense and reconciliation.

It is My Heart's desire to re-unite hearts broken by pain. Pity is not enough. I will knit together the broken places with seams so fine only My eyes will know where the joins are. Scars will be fine ribbons of light, reflecting My love to those

211

with eyes to see. A welcome waits there for those looking to see.

Curiosity will work in everyone's favour.

Those who ask will be answered.

Those who answer will be healed.

All will see the glory established and the love of God revealed in these places of reflective love.

No longer will people seek where they will not find.

They will seek the Truth and be forced to choose, when it is clearly displayed before them. To reject is pure folly. To accept is to receive the Gift of Life, abundant in blessing, mighty in mercy, (to become) acceptable to the Lord of Hosts.

He rides in majesty and all will one day bow down before Him.

His name is Jesus.

Without Him, you can do nothing.

Give praise and honour to His name and let the nations know He is the Chosen One, the One for whom the world waits travailing in labour. Birth pangs are beginning. Watch and see that the finger of the Lord is pointing at the times, and pointing to the places where Love is released and active in His world.

The places are few, the needs many, and more lovers are required.

Is the imposition of Love upon your shoulders?

Would you know?

What would you do if you felt this most precious of burdens?

Would you lay down your lives?

Would you say "Later, Lord?"

212

Would you step aside so the burden fell to the person behind you? If so you would lose your place in the Queue of Life. This is the Armourer's queue, where My army is equipped for battle.

To refuse the armour is to go, unprepared, without protection into the Valley of Death. See for yourselves the folly in this.

To accept the armour is to stop your life, relinquishing the controls and choices which have pleased *you*, in order to please *Me*.

It is a ground shift and you must make the decision.

You alone can make it.

It is *your* life we are speaking of.

Do you want it - or not?

Only those who lay it down will find it again.

Only those who trust Me with their lives will experience the joy of being fully alive. Only those who relinquish their holds will enjoy the fullness of power.

Do not be afraid. I know what I am calling you to.

You may sense - but *I know.* Do you trust Me - enough?

Would I show you anything but My glory?

Would I take you anywhere except to My Father's house?

Would I ask you for anything less than I have already given you?

Trust Me with your life - and you shall see My glory.

Choose. Choose wisely.

I will help those whose courage falters, whose spirit is willing but whose flesh is weak.

Remember I *know* this.

Gethsemane provided for *you* in this way, as My flesh followed my Spirit.

213

I *know* this hard place, but I *established* the path for your feet - *then*. So *choose*. Choose again. Choose wisely.

Seek Me for **My** courage, **My** confidence, **My** reassurance, **My** encouragement, **My** hope, **My** certainty, **My** safety, **My** security. They are yours, for the asking.

Remember - I *know*.

Remember - I *love* – and I do not underestimate the cost. Open your eyes. Count the cost. Pay the price with your life - it is why you were given it.

People need to know this.

The gift of life is a currency to spend in My temple - the place of My Being.

If I will return the tithe sixty- to a hundred-fold, what will I do with a life? **Abundant** life is My promise. Test Me on this. Spend a little of your life and see the increase.

This is no lottery. Everyone's a winner and the jackpot is there for the asking.

Why settle for counterfeit, currency that is void?

Try instead the eternal currency of life -

yours, for Mine.

Your whole life for a heartbeat of Mine.

But, in a heartbeat, I can create universes, smile into oblivion forces of darkness that threaten to overthrow My precious world, heal multitudes, restore *all* that the locusts have stripped from My Creation.

Can you imagine such power?

All the wrongs you've wished to right can be accomplished in the twinkling of an eye, in **My** power, in **My** strength.

So what now of this exchange - your life for Mine?

214

Does it excite you, thrill you, cause you to move nearer to the eternal "Yes" that My heart longs for?

Try Me and see. Try before you buy.

All free offers as I break My body and feed you in loving sacrifice. 1

Do not take lightly the gifts of My Church.2

Do not relinquish the time-honoured truths for spur-of-the-moment novelty. No one can recreate the finest, which I breathed life into.3

No one needs to try. Rest, assured of My goodness, in the places of <u>My</u> making and do not look for Me where man <u>strives</u> to present Me.

I am in the smallest of sighs, the secret whisper of the breaking heart, concealed in the dark places.

I am in the breaking of dawn, the crash of the mighty ocean, the quietness of the mountain slope carpeted in snow.

Struggle to hear Me in the quietness and you will hear My heart-beat.

Watch for Me. I will come, to anoint your brow with kisses, to keep an appointment made in the **Diary of My Heart**.

<u>Watch</u> and <u>see</u> that the Lord is <u>good</u>, is <u>triumphant</u>,
is over all."

215

Wednesday 23 November 2005 10.20pm

"LOVERS CALL WARRIORS...THE DAY OF
THE SMALL PEOPLE"

"And there will come a day when heartbeats will rouse nations, when lovers will call warriors.

Notice LOVERS call WARRIORS.

LOVE leads. Love <u>always</u> leads.

Nothing stands before or against Love that can match its strength, its beauty.

No rivalry can be allowed in My Kingdom and Love reigns supreme.

It is the price of Love which purchases brides.

It is the sound of Love that calls to warriors.

It is the beat of Love that drums the marching of My people.

*People will look for the sound. Where does it come from? - <u>My</u> heart, beating <u>in</u> them, beating <u>for</u> them - but they will hear it as a mighty tornado, ripping up the trees rooted in haste, in shallow ground.*1

Mighty men will topple and 'Giants of God' will count for nothing.

The day of the small people is fast approaching.

You will see them on street corners, in shops, in doorways, in huddles, and they will show you where My Spirit is at work.

You will know this is true because of the anointing I pour

216

over you. You have asked and I have given.

Look not to others, or lean on your own understanding - for I Am sufficient to you.

It is My joy to reveal Myself to you. Seek Me often for we are all going on a journey.

I have vistas to show you and places to reveal where My heart beats with love, in the cold of darkness.

You will enter this darkness and take back what is Mine.

I will show you what and I will show you how.

Rejoice, rejoice. I, the Lord, your God, hear your voices raised to Me. It is My delight to answer you, to bless you, to love you into My heart."

Christmas Eve 2005   9.25am

"YOU ARE WHAT YOU EAT...
I CANNOT BE DISPLACED - I AM"

"A day is coming, is almost upon us, when the hour shall grow dark.

Nowhere will man find light for the Light of the World will look away.

In that moment Heaven shall open and the peal of the Almighty will thunder through the universe. Torn and open heavens will be visible to all as the Light will not be able to be contained.

Streaming from heaven the Light will come.

Dancing in the streets of the capital the Light will illuminate the alleyways of secrets.

Nothing will be hidden any longer and deepest secrets will be forth told. Nowhere will man hide beyond the scrutiny of the piercing eyes of the Holy One.

People will flee to the mountains but the hills will not hide them. Screams will echo round the turrets as the prisoners of their own making are forced to come out.[1]

Walls will fall down and not hold them any more.

Pandemonium [2] will seem familiar but a Word will bring calm. A single Word will be spoken to render harm harmless.[3] Power will go forth in that Word and nations cower before it is spoken over them.

The Word speaks - and no one listens - YET.

The Word beckons - and no one responds.

218

The Word invites - and people turn away.

Alter this with a word made flesh.
The flesh of the Word will consume the people. They will be absorbed by it and taken into It by It. This is the reverse of old ways.

Before, they were invited to chew on the word, but then the Word will feed on them. All that is sweet, He will swallow. All that is bitter He will spit out.

To be spat from the mouth of God is the final rejection and bears no comparison.

Beyond this place, no one will go because here is the very heart of Being. To be part of The Heart, part of the Being, is all that remains for faithful followers. To be drizzled with spittle is a salving experience. To be sweet to the taste blesses God.

Refine your ways. Refine your heart and know that I speak Truth into it.

*You thought you had to make Me fit the places of position₄ but all the time I have been making you **Mine** - **My** lover, **My** friend, **My** consoler, **My** heart throb, **My** Reacher into Darkness, **My** Hope to the Nations, **My** Word to be Spoken.*

You did not know these things and it would have overwhelmed you to think of them. But this is not the case any more.

Through the Path of Brokenness you have travelled a great distance, overcoming enemies and demons of Despair, False Hope and Confusion.

You were not aware of these but at each point of overcoming you had a place to choose - and you chose well.

You chose LIFE.₅ The fruit of your choice is here and now _you_ will taste the sweetness of the Lord, as He savours you on His tongue.

Your sweetness brings joy and you are not to worry about anything, ever again.₆ This is not merely to console you. It is to save time being wasted.

Time has run out for frivolities. **NOW** is the time for battle stations. Warriors need their positions. Yours is in an ailing world where Light is diminishing, fading fast.

You will bring light through LOVE.

To whom would I gift LOVE to be employed, if not you?

Who would apply the lessons of the heart, if not you?

Where else could I go for a faithful, truthful servant, if not to you?

Just as I would have died only for you, so I depend only on you. You are to look to no other servants, only to your self to serve Me. You _are_ _all_ that I have and must live as though all lives depended on you for their salvation. ₇

This is not to overwhelm you, but to strip you of frippery and nonsense.

When you realise the magnitude of this position, you will be sober - and we can begin.

Take time to ponder this. Let the words go to work in you. Know that I, the Lord, _your_ God, watch over you, and yours, and will let no hair of your head be touched.

Walk in fearlessness, _in_ COURAGE, _in_ DELIGHT. Discover what these places look like. _Feel_ the joy they hold. They are resting places and bathing places where restoration and refreshment await those who find them. They are locations for the soul's health and vitality. Enjoy them.

They are for your pleasure.

It is My birthday. It is yours.[8] *Now do you see the importance of My Mother to you? Now do you see why I gave her to you. Notice* **I** *gave her to you - as a birthday present, of reunification. Avail yourself now and step into the fullness of that gift, her presence in your life.*

You will not lose Me, or displace Me. That is **not possible** *- because I Am greater than all.* [9]

Displacement is **NOT possible** *and idolatry is different. Idolatry is placing something between us, so that I Am obscured.* **I CANNOT be DISPLACED.** *I* **AM** *and I do not go away when false idols are placed before Me. I Am simply shut out, rejected, and often lonely for My loved ones. I still long to look on them with love and My Heart aches for those who shut Me out with novelty, distraction, or spirit life of their own making.*

Behind it all I Am still there. I still call - silently. I still wait - patiently. My heart breaks with love - constantly.

Tell My people that **I AM THERE** *- where they need Me - waiting for them to dismantle the constructions they have placed, or allowed, to cloud their vision.*

I CANNOT be DISPLACED. I AM.

When people realise this, they will find it easy to let go of their pain, their hurts, their afflictions, their fears, their longings, their unrequited loves, their unsatisfied needs.
Then, they will see Me, as I smile My love into their desolate hearts.

Help them to remove their emotional blindfolds, by speaking Truth: I **cannot** *be* **DISPLACED.** *I* **CANNOT** *be* **LOST.** *I* **CANNOT be** *rejected or consigned to a place and* *left behind - because I __AM__. And I __AM__ everywhere.*

I am in the trees, in the bird song, in the whine of air moaning violently, in the motion of a body, in the air you breathe. I __AM__. This is __MY__ WORLD.

Man has guardianship but __I own__ it.

It is __MINE.__ __I MADE__ it.

Dispel arrogance with Truth.

Let people know I am calling again - soon, for the last time.

As My voice dies out the blackness will engulf. Only My WORD will lighten this and My WORD will need to be inside people. They will need to have swallowed it, for famine is coming and sustenance will be according to the WORD within.

__BATHE__ in it. WASH in it. FEED on it. __SWALLOW__ it. 10

You are what you eat.

Tell them that the __Day of the Lord is fast approaching.__ __NO__ time to dally or play around with __LIFE.__   __LIFE__ needs __LIVING__ people.   So __LIVE__."

222

Friday 30 December 2005

"TAKE COURAGE FROM THE PLACE OF
FEARLESSNESS...TO THE NATIONS"

"Take courage, from the place of fearlessness. ₁ Take courage to the nations and tell them that I, their Lord, wish that courage was everyone's fruit. It is My gift. I would have My people eat it, feed on it, and consume it. It is the fruit of their bellies - if they will turn to Me.

No longer would loins turn to water, in a world governed by Me. But while government belongs to the misinformed, courage remains a fruit beyond reach. My word says "Do not fear'. It is a command as well as a consoling word, encouraging word. But the misinformed allow fear free access, believing it to be a consequence of circumstance.

It is not. It (fear) is the seed that produces the circumstance and must be uprooted.

Only those with ears to hear will know this.

Open the ears of My people. Unstop the ears that stopped, gave up listening to My Word. Make My Word known, in witness and in TRUTH. Tell the Truth to My people. It is all that I have left to give them, for all has been poured out already in Blood.

If the Truth will not be listened to then all will be lost to them. They need to know this. Leave them in no doubt.

The Place of Fearlessness is not a market place where

223

courage goes to the highest bidder, the best player. It is a place of abiding, where love rules and nurtures, bringing life and hope. It is a place of longing, where the longing is in and of My Heart. It is a place of restoration and revival where all that is needed, in energy and refreshment, is there for the taking. Take it - and take it back to the place of battle. It is needed - and it is enough for the day.

Return at the end of each day and lay down the burdens at the Gate of Remembrance. Step through and in to the pool of Fearlessness. Soak and be washed clean of the traces of burdens.₂ When you are ready, refreshed and rested, return through the Gate. You will find the burdens gone, whisked away by angel hands to be disposed of according to My will. You brought them to Me - the rest is Mine.

*Go out again and repeat the **LIVING**₃ that My tired and aching world requires. Take Me to the nations. Tell them My **TRUTH**. Open the ears of the unhearing. **I** will give you the words that will penetrate deafness and will lift blindness of vision.*

Go and tell them. Ask me for the moment, the occasion, the opportunity. I Am waiting to release them all to you.

Know that I am your Beloved - and you are MINE.

Together, in intimacy, we will travel. Unknown, we will be seen. Unrecognised, we will be welcomed.

Watch and see that I, the Lord, speak the TRUTH - and, in these matters, commit your ways to Me, that I might quickly anoint the path of following for your feet to rest on. Know I love you. Nothing else matters, Beloved."

Friday 24 February 2006

"TODAY'S BREAD...COME TO THE FEAST OF TABERNACLES"

"My heart is poured out on a bleeding and ailing world. Tomorrow, depths of despair shall be plumbed that no-one can imagine. My heart shall surely break if My people do not turn to Me, to ask for succour, to plead for mercy, to forgive the unforgivable.

There is a time coming when doors shall surely be closed and Heaven will close its eyes, unable to look on the terrible things that sin has wrought in the world.

*The minds and thoughts of My people are corrupt. No-one seems to see the **NEED** for **PURITY**. It is a word lost to the nations, unknown to the generations. But without it, no-one can come to ME.*

*This is a time for **REVIVAL** but the price will be high. Torrents of tears will flow, **MUST** flow, to cleanse the hearts and minds of My Beloved. Even those I call 'Dearest' know the state of their hearts.*

Impurity masquerades as so many things: 'good' deeds, 'good' thoughts, 'good' ideas, but unless they are rooted in Me, they are not. They are false - poor imitations of what I would have. And how would they know, those who parade their faith? All around them, others say and affirm, but I don't. No-one asks Me. No-one says *to* Me "Is this the way? because they think they <u>know</u>. But do they? Do they <u>know</u> My ways? C<u>an</u> <u>they</u> know **My** ways? What if I change₁ My mind? Dead habits yield dead works.

    I Am fresh, new every morning.

Today's bread is for <u>today</u> - not tomorrow; and it cannot feed yesterday.
And it cannot be eaten tomorrow, saved for another day.₂
Manna in the desert was a fresh daily blessing, new every morning.
How much fresher is the Bread of Life? ₃
How much fresher can it be than Body to body? ₄

Where are you, My people? Can't you hear Me calling you,
  to come to the **Feast of Tabernacles?** ₅
    <u>My Bread</u> for y<u>ou</u>r tabernacle. ₆
    My Tabernacle for your bread. ₇
I receive, too, into My Tabernacle, the bread of your lives, the sacrifices of your hearts. These <u>feed</u> <u>Me</u> - so nourishment is both ways.
  <u>I</u> feed and nurture well-being into your souls.
  I purify your spirits.
  I soothe and caress your hearts.
  I pour new life into your being, so that **<u>strength</u>** typifies **<u>My</u>** people.

In return, <u>you</u> pour praise and pain into <u>My</u> Tabernacle.
    <u>I</u> receive. <u>I</u> consume. <u>I</u> purify.
I return, whole, hearts that have been offered to Me in brokenness, sacrifice, dying life.

*Where else would you get this **EXCHANGE**?*
Can you not see the magnitude of My gift to you?
*An **EXCHANGE** of life, for death.*
*Y<u>ou</u>r death, <u>My</u> **LIFE**.*

*D<u>aily</u>, this takes place - **NEEDS** to take place.*

My world is corrupt, with death stalking My Beloved. There is nothing to fear. At the place and moment of exchange, all is found. Losses are wiped out, pain is erased, tears are kissed away by kisses from My mouth.
To be in My Heart is to be in the place of understanding, refuge, comfort, consolation, restoration, empowerment, new life and abundant source.
This is the place of Tabernacle.

*<u>Learn.</u> **EAT**! ENJOY the <u>Truth</u>, written here for you to <u>consume</u>. And I will bless your coming in and your going out. And you will be <u>pure</u> vessels in My ailing world, pure enough to take My love and light to those lost in darkness Only ensure that the darkness is not in you, or you in it.*
<u>I</u> am the <u>only</u> place, the only source,
***the ONLY**.*

No-one comes before Me. No anointed ministers can tell of My Heart, because today's bread is new every morning. Only those who enter the Tabernacle of My heart can feed on new bread.

Nourish, or die - the choice is yours."

227

AMEN.

FOOTNOTES

FOOTNOTES

These consist of the specific understanding that accompanied the words, some expansion of definitions and a little background where it seemed appropriate. What I offer here is necessarily partial and not intended to be prescriptive or definitive, since I am only one reader. Reflection leads to more personal understanding. A Bible, a Concordance and a dictionary are invaluable for deeper revelation of the roots and riches of the messages.

1986

'Join The Feast of Salvation' 5 April
1   The first words from the Lord, after waking suddenly for the second night at 3am.
2   *'salvation'* means: the act of saving; the means of preservation from any serious evil; the saving of man from the power and penalty of sin; the conferring of eternal happiness. (Chambers Dictionary)
NB. Bible definition more fruitful.

'Love -The River /Ocean of Timeless Love'27 July
1   *"..all your burdens.."* - include: personal troubles and the offences against us; and our concerns for other people.
2   *"...even others."* - refers to intercession and people bathing in, and trustfully releasing their burdens into, Love. Sometimes we listen to those whose hearts are heavy with concern for people known only to them. If we become 'living springs' where they can release their burdens into the 'flow of love', our then combined love can flow more powerfully to carry those concerns/'others' towards assured healing in God, who is Love.

'Into the Mouths of Children' 1 January

1   *"...from the mouths of babes.* -indicates this new generation of children will somehow be significant in God's plan, as worshippers who recognise Him. The efficient world we know will not satisfy them and they will find their joy in the Lord.

'From the Forehead of Your Son' 2 January

1   *"From forehead..star of light.."* - the *'star'* is explained in later pieces as an obvious sign of a life-long follower of the Lord. Perhaps it is the presence of God that shines from some believers' faces.

(At this time, my younger son Adam is twenty months; but at eighteen years old, Adam has a powerful and dramatic experience of God, joining others of his generation to live a worshipping lifestyle that fulfils the previous prophetic message.)

2   *"..the first angel, the first horn."* Can this be Revelation 8 v.7?

'Mary is the Mother of My Child' 24 October

1.   During prayer the Lord instructed me to: *"Open your hands to receive the blessings of the Lord. Open your heart to receive the blessings of the Lord's Word. SERVE Me. KNOW ME as your LORD."* He had my complete attention then and continued seamlessly with the words about Mary.

If He had started with Mary, I probably would have stopped listening; because these words and understanding came at a time when I was cautious about Mary and had completely sidelined her beyond my chosen spiritual spotlight. I could not receive them for many years, until 1999, because I remained untrusting and therefore prejudiced.

2 " *- a sceptre of peace in an age of darkness."*- Only the King holds out

the sceptre to His subjects.

3 *"Her beauty shines forth today."*.-Her beauty is definitive, contributive and current. It is unchanging and unaffected by onslaught; and, as such, is an example of hope and light in darkness.

4 *"..even amid the torrents and deluge of abuse that fall from unsuspecting mouths."* - People can denigrate Mary, or her significance, through ignorance; but they cannot eliminate her presence, which He later describes as a bestowed *"token of (His) great love"*.

5 *"For to whom would I entrust My precious mother if not to those who would reverence and care for her?"* - Jesus calls His mother *'precious'* and He is protective of her, careful to entrust her only to those who would treat her in a way that He considers appropriate, i.e. with high respect and regard. As Son of God, He shows us the right, human way to treat our own mothers.

6 *"..through her, many more thousands will come to Me."*- Mary <u>always</u> points to Jesus. Since receiving this message, many thousands have responded to Mary at Medjugorge in Croatia, embracing her call to **full conversion to Jesus,** through: repentance, Scripture, prayer from the heart - (including biblical Rosary meditations on the life of Christ, for those who can accept this prayer model) - fasting, and Holy Communion. These are called the 'stones to slay Goliath'; i.e. offensive weapons of spiritual warfare.

7 *"..she is a way of truth, ..beauty, ..justice, within which captives flourish."*- People who are helpless, trapped, impotent, bound, can still thrive fearlessly. Mary's responses to what God asked of her set a faithful example that liberates.

233

8   *"When they cannot find the Way, they can find a mother's arms.."* - means: every baby is born to a woman and cannot resist their loving mother's arms. In a spiritual sense, Mary acts as our spiritual mother and her role is to carry in her motherly arms those who need, but cannot yet look for, or find, Jesus. She carries them to Jesus, or turns them to face Him, if they are looking in the wrong direction. Either way, they are brought to, or enabled to see and focus on, <u>Him</u> - <u>always</u> on **Him**. Their hurting and hungry spirits cannot resist her because she is the loving spiritual mother; and she continues to serve her Son's wishes, as she would have done on earth.
That makes her an invaluable spiritual asset when praying for 'lost' people.
Her motherliness was indomitable - Scripture records her physical presence at the foot of the cross, watching her son die. That makes her a fore-runner for every mother's fears and experiences; and therefore a potential source of inspiration, even for those who cannot receive her as *'a token'* of Jesus' love.

9   *"But she lost yours first...restoring you to her arms."* - a personal reference to the damaging emotional consequences of a two-year separation from my mother from the age of 5, when I was admitted to hospital with incurable chronic kidney disease.

10   *"I offer you the arms of My mother...restored to the baby."* - if I would let Mary mother me spiritually, I would then be able to receive mothering from **my** mother, thereby facilitating the restoration of motherhood to my deprived mother. Twelve years later this word came true after the disruption of a murder rendered me defenceless. I was restored to my mother's 'arms' for three months before she died.

11   *"I would have you know Me as...lover.."* - To know Jesus as 'lover' was a startling, new concept to me in 1987; and it took a long time,

234

therefore, for me to trust the whole message. The message of intimacy with Jesus has since become widespread through many sources, including the ministry of Mike Bickle, from the International House of Prayer, in Kansas, U.S.A.

12 *"..yield the first fruits...path of sacrifice"*- Refers to events ahead that would require letting go of something important in order to move forward through the changes. I was in a family- and life-building phase, so letting go of anything I was working to put together was an alien concept. Although I didn't understand it at the time, God was trying to prepare me for a fuller, better life.

<u>1988</u>

'The Tree of Life' 30 April
1 *".. the hurt enamoured of Me"*   -   this hurt is not destructive as it is valued by God and full of His love and presence. He will be fully present in the experience and sense of brokenness, giving confidence to the broken to accept His refining.

2 *"Mary will help this passage to My heart..."* - This might offend some people's dogma; and, in terms of the book, it would have been easier for me if the Lord had not said it, because I have to contend with reactions – occasionally particularly hostile from those whose beliefs exclude her from the spiritual landscape.
But He has His reasons and I can only be truthful and present what I have been given, describing how it affected me. Readers must decide for themselves.
   This reference to Mary was a serious challenge to me, which I mulled over. Two days later I decided that entering God's heart was more important than misgivings; and I sensed a message that was from somewhere outside me: *'Prayer and fasting every Friday for suffering humanity is the way into the Lord's heart'*. I did not hear it in the way He speaks from my heart. I <u>felt</u> it was from Mary, but

didn't want to give that any thought. I reasoned that sacrificial prayer and fasting for '*suffering humanity*' could be a good thing anyway – and if it took me into His heart, so much the better. If not, it was a small gift to offer to Jesus.

'The Coming of My Kingdom Will Be Upon The Land.'
19 October

1   "*..stand firm by bathing in My Word, whose presence*" - Bathing in Jesus will give firm footing in troubled times. Soaking in the living Word of scripture will wash our minds and give us clear vision of right and wrong in God's terms. Standing on His 'right' teaching gives us anchored stability, especially in a changing, relative world.

2   " *..a good and faithful servant...*" - will be an agent of change for the Lord.

3   "*Be ready for the Day of Judgement. Weep and lament for the forgotten ones whose families leave them in the throes of Hell.*" - This is a reference to those who have died and whose surviving family have consigned them to death / Hell as though that is the end of them. It seems from this that they are not finished with; but could be forgotten, by those who could think that death is the end and / or no further redemption possible.

This clearly speaks of existence after death. It is an exhortation to remember and intercede in some active way for the '*forgotten*' ones who are both dead in a worldly sense and everlastingly alive. They need not, nor must not, be forgotten yet; and it is an indication of hope that they still have existence, although in a place of suffering.

It is a plea for compassion and love, to actively cry out for those '*forgotten ones*' - perhaps also from previous generations? Could those currently languishing in Hell be rescued, or their torment relieved in some way, by sorrowing intercessors, before the '*Day of Judgement*'?

It seems that families could have another chance to '*weep and lament'* if they want it; but purposefully, out of love for their departed ones, and not in sorrow for themselves.

And we, too, must all be moved by the plight of those *"forgotten ones'* with no one to care about them.

1989

'Love Call'   21 February

1 *"My life alone is for you"* - is sufficient

2 *"Love me alone"* - before everyone else; in first place

3 *"In all things know My name"* - bring the name of Jesus, His love, power and presence, into every situation; thereby also introducing *salvation* (see Footnotes1986: 2).

4 *"No sin can separate us"*- if we truly repent and tell Him everything, no sin is too big or awful to keep us apart from Jesus.

5 *"My life for you alone"* - His gift of redemption is so *personal* that Jesus would have gone to the cross, to save us from our sin, if any *one* of us had been the *only* one on earth.

6 *"No guilty conscience"* - do not let guilt overwhelm you or come between you and Jesus.

7 *"..life's false charms"* - everything we have tried and preferred to Him.

'DIARY of THE LORD' commission 18 March

1   I was cleaning the bath, trying to quickly finish housework before collecting my children from nursery and school, when I sensed the Lord say *"Stop! Take up your pen and write..."*. I dropped the cloth, ran into the bedroom, grabbed something to write on and wrote these first words. The rest of the command about this book then followed. I did not know if the specific name was a real

237

publisher and I decided <u>not</u> to find out, because if they did <u>not</u> exist, I was losing my mind; but if they <u>were</u> real, GOD had DEFINITELY just spoken to me! Either way, I was seriously alarmed. Three month later, in a startling way, I discovered the publishers actually exist.

2   To date (2008) the publishers have not wanted to read any of the book and I have not told them about God's instruction. When things change, readers will see God's will in this accomplished, because I will celebrate it on the website *www.diaryofthelord.com* People who have known about the *'DIARY'* since 2003 are able to verify the name of God's chosen publishers, whose letter is also on file. I am not free to offer *'DIARY of the LORD'* to any other publisher, for obvious reasons; but I am distributing it according to His instruction to me, preceding the named publishers' involvement.

'Give...Act in Love'   19 September
1   *"In such as these My heart beats..."* - The Lord's heart beats in those who ask or demand God's love from us; so how can we refuse anyone, or give short measure, curtail their demands, or announce the personal cost to ourselves? There is no need to feel overwhelmed by demand if we follow His guidelines in *'Love - the River/ Ocean of Timeless Love'* 1986.

2   *"The lowly are...scattered for...my people"* - People needing God's love expressed through gifts of understanding, time, sustenance, protection and aid, are scattered throughout societies and countries. Often despised and rejected, God calls them His princes, because their very needs call on our compassion, developing it and making sure that it never becomes redundant. The 'lowly' herald and occupy His kingdom on earth, serving His purposes and rightfully calling on us to respond appropriately to their needs.

3   *"..daily feeding of My Word, in print and in flesh, where possible.."* means that we need to consume Jesus in scripture and in Eucharist (the sacramental breaking and sharing of consecrated bread in memory of the Lord's Supper) every day, where possible; NB 'Give us this day our daily bread' – from the prayer Jesus taught His disciples, commonly called the 'Our Father' or 'The Lord's Prayer' Luke 11 v.3.

4. *"All glory to Me...that I might blemish the sullied past"* - Restore God to His rightful first place, then He will destroy our sinful idolatrous past and bring a free future that will glorify Him and bless us.

'Take My Love To The Prisoners/A Day of Anointing Is At Hand' 7 November

A profound, commanding word about His **LOVE** in action.

1   *"..in a voice of woe.."* Despite the *sound* or appearance of misfortune, only joy is waiting if people will seek Him. Joy is not happiness, but is a rejoicing that comes from knowing God is in charge of our lives, our world, our future. With that certainty, His gift of joy is released in times of woe as strength to those who seek Him. He will use times, or *'a voice'*, of woe to draw people to Him; giving them opportunity to realign their lives, or deepen their relationship, with Him.

2. *"Yield to Me a nation of free men.."* - take His love to all prisoners, setting their spirits free.

'Purify yourselves' 29 December

1   *"Purify yourselves...trapped soul."* Jesus has already suffered in advance and paid the full price for our sins, yet is inviting us to make reparation by seeking to comfort His heart. This is to be

239

drawn into a safe Love, a healing place of perfect peace, as a way of finding rest from the sin we turn away from. This will *'strip us of the world's offerings', 'purify'* us and make us *'whole'* in His sight.

Comforting His heart in this way not only brings us healing, but somehow He offers a consequential connection for the sake of the souls of the departed: He receives comfort from us, which releases His redeeming love for them. He wants us to do our part, so that He can then do His -*"My heart is full of their need and My people need to be ready to rescue them."* (**NB** *'The Coming of My Kingdom'*1988)

Love, it seems, is full of mystery and power, connected in ways beyond our understanding.

2. *"..***not My will** *that they are prisoners of the mind, or of the body...that they perish in a sea of uncertainty, or confusion, or insecurity, or doubt. ...invite Me in."* - God does **not** want **mental** or **physical** incapacity. Only He offers completeness and wholeness - all other help and efforts definitely fall short of His perfection; and to the individual who wants *"health of mind and body"* He says *"Invite me in."* Jesus is the answer, the cure, the fulfilment of the empty spaces.

1990

'I Do Preside' 15 August

1   *"Loss...will incur disbelief in the eyes and hearts of My followers - "*

Even His followers can be pushed by life experiences and events to the brink of disbelief. We see pointless waste, experience shocking loss. 'How can God be real, be loving and let these things happen?' is a cry of desperation. The temptation then is to refuse to have anything to do with a God who seemingly will not prevent catastrophe.   Sometimes faith has to be blind, when it is being pushed to the next level. It is then a choice between *temptation* to reject Him and *Truth*.

240

Scripture is full of His presence and His promises never to leave us, so do we stay with our loss and desperation, letting pain lead us into stubbornness; or, despite the blinding pain or anger, choose His Word and His overcoming strength to carry us and others through everything, to His place of *'new order'*?

2   *"Develop your obedient spirit, unburdened by binding, yet compliant to My will."*

When our spirits are released and healed from the burden of sin, its wounds, restrictions, deep hurts, compulsions and any ungodly ties, we are free. God wants us to actively participate in developing our freed spirit, so that we become obedient and freely responsive to His will.

'Compliant' means yielding, flexible, submissive, agreeing. We will want this from our heart, if we spend time with Him and let Him love us to wholeness.

"I Am the Refiner"   9 November
1.   *"No change can take place unless people let go-"*
We can become bound to many things, which may then govern us.

<u>1991</u>

"Take time...Master Craftsman.." 7 September
1.   *"No longer seek the ways...fall away from you."* God alone forms us. This is a warning not to model our faith walk on anyone else. We can be inspired by others, but only to turn more deeply to Jesus. We do not conform to the personality of leaders themselves, although we can be shepherded through their anointed authority.

2   *"I mould and fashion in My own design."* Only God knows how He wants us to develop.

3   *"..outside"* refers to the physical body; *"inside"* refers to mind and spirit. (At this time, in September 1991, I had just been diagnosed with M.E. (myalgic encephalomyelitis), which had followed an extreme bout of chicken-pox and viral pneumonia the previous Easter. As I learned to spend time with the Lord, letting Him work in me – including obeying His call to receive daily Eucharist as soon and as often as I could - He brought me to complete physical healing within two years.)

4. *"He is hearing My voice"* - My husband was baptised at 21, sixteen years before I met him. He has never been a 'talk the talk' Christian; but is a man of unlimited love, patience, compassion and kindness, who 'walks the walk'.

In our early years together, to my immature and anxious mind, I was a 'solitary' believer in need of a remodelled husband who would conform to what I had learned was the Christian prototype husband – someone who would pray with me and 'cover' me.

I did not know then that Jesus was reserving that position for Himself.

Meanwhile, He was assuring me that the indubitable goodness in my husband was the fruit of the Spirit's voice guiding him – even though he might seem oblivious to it.

5. *"Honour him in all things...in your house."* Honouring my husband, in all things - God promised here - would bring His glory into our house. This is a simple lesson for every woman; relieving, too, so much trouble caused by conflicting perceptions and critical judgement. But it flies in the face of many cultural influences, requiring change for many world-hardened women.

I am still trying to learn how to do it – and, as a consequence of my slow growth, my husband now shows even more forbearance, mercy and beautiful humility.

On an expanded level, could it mean that God's glory would fill the 'house' where due respect and honour were given to those in authority? What could happen if churches, work-places, schools, media, etc., manifest respect instead of complaint, criticism and opinionated struggle – would God respond sovereignly and His glory bring what was needed to make those places, and the lives of people in them, fruitful and peaceful?

"I Am a Personal God." 21 September 5.40pm
1. *"Come forth and be disrobed of your grave clothes."* He is calling us out of our tombs of comfort zones and inward looking habits, with an invitation to be loosed from the trappings of dead thoughts and practices.

2. *"I do not need you in a service, or a congregation, or a praise gathering, or a worship meeting."* - These are not redundant, but secondary to the Lord's primary place of meeting, which He names as the individual's heart.
3 *"..a suffering of the Spirit and a transforming of the heart."* We are called to let Him live and rule in our hearts, bringing healing and change to us; and to allow the Holy Spirit to move us to pray for things that matter to God, in any form of expression He chooses. He transforms our hearts in the process. Because God is Love, any transformation is **pure** gift.

'Purity / I Am the Harvester..the Restorer' 18 November
   Important words of **Sacrifice** and **Purity**.
1. *"Purity is the cutting edge of My sword of the Spirit. It blazes towards Heaven, drawing down Heaven's power to dispel and vanquish the evil hordes that crowd around men, polluting the atmosphere of My creation."* - God's sword of the Spirit is the Word of God and Purity is its cutting edge.
   Purity on earth draws down Heaven's power to scatter and

overcome the oppressive forces of evil that crowd around us and pollute all God's creation, both material and invisible. If we wish to overcome and establish victory in our own lives, or for others, we need to wield the sword and keep its cutting edge sharpened by the Lord.

Reading the Word of God washes and purifies us, giving us a cutting edge for the rubbish in our lives and a source of power to overcome all evil. And if we are purified, we can be used as God's cutting edge and a sign of His power for others.

2.   *"I would have a pure world where symptoms of madness and confusion disappear".* PURITY is the antidote to such symptoms. It is not His will that people suffer from such corruptions. Washing our minds in the Word brings purity by softening us and showing us where we are out of line with God, so encouraging us to repentance. His Word seeds in us and also waters our dry places, making us grow healthily and become fruitful.

<u>1992</u>

"I Am Lord" 28 March

1.   *"..it is in giving that you receive."*

We must not hoard God's blessings or we become spiritual misers. Our blessings, material or spiritual, are also God's food for the starving and lost. He trusts us to share.

This is a commanding and rebuking appeal, perpetually challenging self-centred spiritual gluttony; and the 'holy huddle' temptations that can creep in and turn church into inward-looking clubs that take the motion out of mission.

If we can humbly accept appropriate challenge and correction, without falling into condemnation or self-justification, we will also hear His heart-rending plea for our hearts to become open-ended; so to receive from God and allow Him to <u>move</u> His blessings through us to those <u>He</u> chooses.

244

1993

No received messages, but a 'Master Class' in GRACE from August1993 to mid-January 1994.

Mark, a 25 year old Buddhist, liked the *'DIARY'* messages he read and added: *"I'd like contextual background stuff, because it would help people know the path that was walked and lived through, while it was being written. They'd know it was real then and it would help them."*

So here, briefly, is a little of the reality that I lived through when God did not give words, but <u>demonstrated</u> that He was in control of life and was better at it than I could ever be.

I was an experienced 'coper', until this time, inclined to gird my <u>self</u> and ask for His <u>help</u> to manage or survive difficulties. He showed me a better way - through too many things for me to deal with; a time that was so full of trouble for <u>all</u> my nearest and dearest that all I could do was prayerfully put on the armour of God (Ephesians 6 vv. 13-19) and ask for the grace to stand. I <u>chose</u> to stand at the centre, to care as well as I could for my family; but God alone enabled me to stand. I watched as <u>He</u> worked things out; and He taught me the <u>best</u> way to live. This was a 'Master Class' in GRACE.

In an unbroken sequence lasting just less than five months from the end of August until mid-January, and set against a backdrop of living next to the 'neighbours from Hell', the following happened in this order:

death of a most dear elderly friend, who had been a mother figure to me for eighteen years; my twelve year old son bullied in school; father-in-law taken to death's door twice in a month; mother-in-law physically ill through stress; husband contracted notifiable infection through job and off-sick for several weeks; another friend died; my younger 9 year old son badly mistreated by a cruel teacher, resulting in a severe asthma attack (offence acknowledged

245

at a disciplinary level); husband suffered suspected coronary attack in work; widowed mother has serious emotional breakdown in Wales and also needs to be moved to a place of safety; husband, aged 49, subsequently ordered to retire from career working with emotionally and behaviourally disturbed children, as doctor fears another such unheralded stress attack could be fatal; god-daughter dies from breast cancer.

I was the only one in my close family that nothing personally happened to.

God had warned me in1986 that some trial was coming up for me; but I knew in the first month that this was not the time He meant.   Instead this was a grace-filled, peace-blessed, <u>hard</u> preparation that improved my relationship with God by teaching me that I <u>could</u> rely and lean on Him in <u>all</u> situations. This is a foundational truth that was paramount to my survival of the trial when it did come, at the turn of the millennium.

1994
'..Precious to Me, Beloved' 15 January
1   *"..an overfilled heart.."* - full of care

1995

I asked God where He was and He answered me immediately with the next two pieces.

"Where are you, God?" Palm Sunday 9 April 10.05 am
1.   *"Hoping for an invitation to the feast of entertainment which blinds My people"*- this refers to church meetings where <u>performance</u> is the skewed focus for people. Their eyes are blinded by the <u>entertaining</u> church, where the congregation *watches* the staged 'worship' and 'almost celebrity' speakers. Sometimes Jesus is not even <u>invited</u>

246

there - so He stands at the gate, hoping and waiting patiently to come in, to be noticed.

"Repentance in the Shadows" Palm Sunday
9 April 10.40 am

1.   *"No bruise or blemish...cared for"* - no imperfection matters when the Lord's concern is to tend us.

....

After reading these messages, I then asked what I <u>could</u> ask Him for, as I wanted to only ask Him for what He wanted to give me. I was trying to come as close to my Father as I could get. He replied:

"Father, what can I ask you for?" Palm Sunday
9 April 11.10 am

1.   *"You can ask Me for....v.2 "the sighs of the lonely"* to *v.3 "lost and lonely"* - this is intercession for others.
2.   He **IS** ALL these things!

1996

"I Am Coming" 25 June

God blesses those who obey His command to put Him first, because His plans are to prosper us. Development and achievement are markers in everyone's life; and an obedient believer can expect their primary growth in God to be reflected in their expanding humanity, as well as in talents, gifts and physical circumstances. Such progress, however, is not dependent on any society's definitions or values.

1.   *"Slaying the dragon of success which haunts and ravages My world"* - Accomplishment has always been part of God's plans for people, according to <u>His </u>will and purpose. But here, the *'dragon'* is the Godless world's idea of progress and achievement that confers enticing or compromising status and brings corrupting worldly

247

rewards. It causes individual people, organisations, governments, to view themselves 'winners/losers' or as a 'success'/ a 'failure' in their own, changing terms; and can lead to an 'ends justify the means' attitude, where dishonesty can enter.

Such self-definition drives people towards idolatrous worldly goals and systems that ultimately raise up the individual/ organisation/ government/ country, etcetera as their own resource and power pack.

If people accept the world's definitions they can become, at the very least, psychologically yoked and economically bound into its secular systems.

Pride, greed and self-centredness flourish in this kind of seductive, 'successful' environment; while self-rejection, despair, loss, possibly even self-destruction, can accompany the world's evaluation of a 'failure'. Sometimes the world's ideas infiltrate church organisation, too.

All of this contradicts God's intentions for His creation and robs people of their God-designed prosperity; so He is promising to *'slay the dragon'*. The dragon's constructions and systems will therefore also collapse.

Scripture charts the destruction of all enemy activity; so even the worldly-wise who reject God can have the chance to reason the outcome of Godless foundations and false rewards.

2.   I asked the Lord to confirm this through Scripture and I was directed to Revelation 3 v.11 : *"I am coming soon; hold fast to what you have, and let no-one rob you of your crown."*

<u>1997</u>

"I Was There in the Summer"

"I led you on" - God does not lead us on to wrong paths, but even if we choose the wrong way, He will not leave us alone.

Jesus accompanies us and will go ahead of us; ready for us to look at Him from the place we find ourselves in; offering Himself as an alternative Way, at every point of decision on the self-directed path. No matter how desperate it feels, He's there already – with gifts of forgiveness and healing - just waiting to welcome, receive and rescue us from our wrong choices.

<u>1999</u>

"Set Aside" 9 May
1.   *".. a foothold in the avalanche of life"* - Life can suddenly change and lose it's shape, through many outside influences. Are we prepared?

<u>2000</u>

"I Am the Moment / A Holy Marriage Awaits.." 19 December

The first message after nineteen months; (the last thirteen months were the most traumatic of my life).   Although this spoke specifically into personal areas, the explicit revelation of <u>how</u> God loves is His encouraging gift for everyone.
1.   *"..sufferings have been real and of account"* validated traumatic effects that had tempted me to think there was something wrong with me that I had been so badly affected by events that others had apparently recovered from. But, to God too, the effects were real and actually mattered.

2.   *"Pain is real...and deeply moving."*   God is moved by our pain.
3.   *"Come into the wilderness, My child."* Wilderness is a pathless, unexplored region, a place where the spirit feels desolate. It is not a place to fear, because the Lord sees it as an opportunity where a holy marriage can take place and be consummated.

4.   *"Yours are safe."* He freed me to be in the wilderness when He

relieved me of my extreme sense of responsibility for my family's safety – an exaggerated emotional response to a closely encountered murder a year before that had been followed three months later by my mother being found dead. The Lord assured me my family were safe without my help, because of HIS love for them.

In the letting go, I discovered relief in emotional freefall. I was past caring then about anything, including what happened to me next.

5. *"I am faithful. I am true. I am steadfast. I am_you."* - if we can recognise qualities such as these in our character, they indicate not just His influence, but **His presence with** us; the presence of the qualities express <u>Him</u>. So, at times of personal need or collapse, He will not disappear, even if we are forced to let go of our positions. He will take our place and express what is needed, in His way. We <u>can</u> trust Him for this.

6. *"Pour yourself into Me.."*- **He** wants to be one with us, **through us pouring ourselves into Him**. This movement of <u>lesser</u> 'pouring into' <u>greater</u> is an action reflected in nature, through the process of osmosis; and it challenges the popular perception and highly vocalised appeals that invite Him to pour Himself into us.

7. *"..even though you walked in clouds of unknowing."*- We can let life, trauma, false attractions blind us to Him and then meander down dead ends. Temptation might try to destroy our faith, but to reject God is a <u>choice</u>.

<u>2001</u>

"I Am the Author of Life"   20 May

1. *"Take them in your heart."*- If we let Him speak His Word into our hearts, He will write His life there for us to live it.

250

2.   *"I will write songs of love, pure joy..."*- the joy of the Lord is our strength and is His antidote to the bleakness and barrenness of so many lives. He wants to write joy into our hearts so that we have it to draw on and share.

The message also foretells the songs *'Come to the Wedding!'* and *'Speak to My World!'*

3. Awesome, Sovereign God!

4.   *"Turn...to the longings of your heart, to know MY longings for you."* The unique, <u>deepest</u>, earliest longings of our hearts can be denied - buried by life's avalanches, forbidden by authority figures, bound by fear, or perhaps lost through hopelessness or discouragement. If we can allow ourselves to find them again, they can tell us something of God's heart,<u> purpose</u> and direction for our lives.

"Come to the Wedding!"13 July (Songs of Joy/ Hope - 1)
1.   v.3 *"My child you can smile....to an end"* - I had a sense this is an invitation to a dying person. It applies in spiritual terms to someone who is facing new life in Jesus; whether for the first time, or at any other stage of breakthrough, including passing from the earth. There is <u>always</u> a bright future in Christ.

2.   v.3 *"..as <u>we</u> tend"* - means working in close partnership with the Lord, as *"we tend the lives of the needy.."*. Working with Jesus in this way means abiding with Him in *'Peace, Joy and Love'* and distributing these gifts to hurting others who are fearful, grief-stricken, troubled, deceived and betrayed.

3.   These words helped a terminally ill lady (unknown to me) prepare to go to the Lord; and formed part of her funeral arrangements a couple of months later.

"Speak to My World!" 23 August (Songs of Joy/Hope - 2)

1.　*'The Day of the Lord'* - refers to the very first message of Love and salvation, which we are told to tell the world, using music and singing. This is a commission. Are there any songwriters and musicians reading this?

2.　*"It's time...To surrender your shame."* Shame conceals and is a resting place for fear to reside in people. When shame is brought to the light of God's waiting love and forgiveness, fear loses its supporting platform.

3.　*"The fear that you carry...of pain."* - Fear <u>must</u> leave when Jesus speaks, taking <u>all</u> attendant pain. I did not see the prophetic message in this at the time, but I experienced its exact fulfilment three months later; when someone used their Christ authority and commanded deliverance in His name.

"Speak out.."Sunday　24 November

1. After I was woken up at 8am by internally 'hearing' these words being emphatically repeated, I could also 'see' them, as on a banner.

　　This released me to start copying up all the messages from the scraps of paper and backs of old envelopes that they were scribbled on; and it came after the healing and prophecy at the previous day's Women's Day of Prayer at King's Church, Narberth, West Wales, when a visiting speaker – Brenda Taylor – ministered to me. Without my explaining anything, she spoke **eleven words of command**, in Jesus' name, and I was **instantly** set free from three years of trauma, caused by the spiritual oppression of shock and sorrow. Praise God for obedient servants who exercise the gift of discernment! And for churches who welcome the healing Holy Spirit.

NB. <u>Four days later the Lord showed me that the scribbled writings</u>

were for His book <u>_'DIARY of THE LORD'._</u>

"I Am Coming - Look"   **10 December**   *
The <u>first</u> piece of the new phase of listening.

"Desire Me / Repent of Lost Ways" 13   December*
Belongs with the preceding and following two pieces.
1.   _'dragon of discontent'_ – a dragon is fierce, intimidating and
watchful, protective of it's possessions; and savage when disturbed
or when it's possessions could be removed.

Discontent is <u>non-satisfaction</u> and its deliberate, exhausting aim
is to **destroy** peace and harmony, (in favour of the detached
counterfeits - passivity and complacency); and **distract** people from
God. It can be masked to look e.g. like goal setting, material
acquisition for the sake of it, obsessive self-improvement, driven
career paths, the surge towards modernising religion in a way that
conflicts with God's Word, to identify but a few faces.

People can feel discontented by social peers, media influences,
family demands; or be caught up in the pressure of systems of
employment, legal requirements, prescribed attainment targets; or
enticed by the sheer attraction of increasing wealth or pursuing
power - to name just some. Governments can even participate,
enshrining 'national targets' that stretch into our everyday lives;
using prescriptive phrases like 'driving up standards' that penetrate
national vocabulary and alter people's concepts, transforming their
values and judgements.

'Performance' can then replace the slower, admirable concept of
'fulfilling potential', almost without notice – removing also the
opportunity and vital responsibility to question the meaning,
consequences and ultimate value of the demanded 'higher'
standards. But 'performance' is not <u>established</u> ability and
'expansion' is not <u>rooted</u> growth.

Those without a solid core can be swept into a current of constant,
accelerating change. 'Switching off' from constant demands can

become a survival strategy; and detachment becomes a characteristic of growing, unresponsive passivity and complacency – with, or without, the person's awareness. The *'dragon'* amasses his treasure.

Life is not always easy or pleasant and can become exhausting; then stress can manifest, be diversionary and become ultimately idolatrous.

People can then lose sight of God -- if they ever knew Him - and ultimately rebel against Him, rejecting His wisdom and His love, considering Him redundant or unreal, in the 'modern' world.

Yet oppose or challenge conventional wisdom, when it fails people, and the 'dragon' stirs. People get dismissed, failed students falter without direction, goal posts shift, important mistakes get hidden, insecurity and fear seep into the national temperament, and so on.

Hard heartedness and thicker skins become the psychological and social shields. People everywhere then suffer, even those trying to follow God.

But, whatever 'correct' opinion says, there is a spiritual force at work behind discontent and the Lord says He will slay it.

2.   *"Repent of lost ways."* - Turn away from life styles that exclude God, because they are 'lost' to Him and everything He offers. Develop a new Love relationship with Him that equips us to resist the conforming pressures of the world, such as the *'dragon of discontent'*.

2003

"I Am Coming - Soon"   23 January*
1. *"Let all...be reconciled"* - is a call to UNITY of believers.
2. *"who hinders the cry of a child"* - we must help, pray (see **'Prayer'**
28 October 1991); and <u>respond,</u> seeking <u>His</u> ways of rescue and bringing peace.

"I Am Coming Soon - I Am Truth"   8 April*
* These all belong together, comprising an URGENT call.

"Fools for the Lord"   8 October
1.   *"...the feet of the wicked...the feet of the lost...monstrosities defiled by self-inflicted wounds who will walk My path."* - These are the people, (later described as those who have been rejected by fearful, oppressed, hard-hearted believers), who are already beyond the safety of the churches. God is CALLING them; and choosing <u>them</u> for this work of evangelism. He is nominating the rejected, to bring in the rejected and lost.
When <u>they</u> receive the truth of Jesus, they will be perfectly placed to spread the gospel by reaching out to others in the same predicaments to tell them of the Lord. They, and anyone else from the churches who respond to this call, will become Fools for the Lord with all that that involves.

2.   *"..callousness is ...a defence grown by oppression."* - means that many of us who are alarmed by e.g. events, people or reports in our daily lives can experience a tension, an emotional 'block'; which gets added to by more oppression, until it is reinforced and forms a barrier which we think will protect us from that which upsets us. In this way we form defensive attitudes to others, to situations, to world problems, etc. Media refers to it as 'compassion fatigue', 'prejudice', 'intolerance', 'racism', 'political correctness' etcetera., depending on the particular circumstances. But, what keeps things *out*, also locks us and our inspiration *in*.

3.   The Lord understands and is compassionate about our trials. He wants us to melt so that His *"fingers of love can retrace...hearts"* i.e. He will rewrite our responses so that we become defencelessly loving and He can use us to reach the lost and untouched. He offers us an alternative to self-defence:

4.   *"Abandon yourself to Me."* He says He knows that this is a fearful challenge; and I understood it as something like playing the old-fashioned trust game, where you fall backwards into someone's arms, believing them to be there to catch you, even though you can't see them. God assures us in Scripture that He will 'never leave ... or forsake' us, so He *will* catch us when we experience oppression in our lives, if we will only fall back into His arms, which we know to be loving and strong. From the completely safe position of being held by Him, we can look all oppression in the face and laugh its comparative feebleness away. From His arms, we then also become enlightened and emboldened, as we begin to recognise the face and strategy of oppression which is intent on closing us down.

He continues by emphasising the difference between holy fear of Him and corrupting fear.

Corrupting fear *"slips in behind man-made defences"*. If we have inadvertently or deliberately created our own blocking defences, we have unwittingly also created a resting place for corrupting fear within ourselves - the major attacking, wounding and binding weapon of the enemy. It corrupts us then by producing a sense of fear as a reaction, maybe even in time becoming an automatic response. The fear base spreads and expands into other areas of our lives, perhaps producing general stress and anxiety, which can be cranked up by any number of things and then also manifest in physical and mental health problems. We may then think we have numerous problems, whereas we could probably only have one root- Fear.

God does not want us to live in fear or be governed by it. That is not only for our good, but also because it stops us loving those we have to date considered unlovable or beyond us.

So our choice is clear: self-defensive blocks which lead to callousness; or abandonment to Him - which leads where?

He says in this message that if we will abandon ourselves to Him, we <u>will</u> be able to reach the lost and the aimless, but we will then also become *'Fools for the Lord'*. The choice is ours. We are at a *'crossroad'* and we may choose. Always we may choose. If we want to see his glory, we need to follow Him.

Jeremiah 6 v.16: *"Stand at the crossroad and look: ask for the ancient paths, ask where the good way is and walk in it and you will find rest for your souls."*

"A Fear-Free World"   17 October

1.   *"..beloved of My mother, .."* - I understood that this brings Mary into the frame because: if we are in relationship with Jesus, <u>He</u> brings us into relationship with 'Our' Father, as adopted children and co-heirs. As adopted children we are, through Jesus, <u>offered</u> the <u>privilege</u> of full relationship in His family. So we become *"beloved of My mother"*. Mary, everlastingly the mother of Jesus, loves us too, because of our relationship with her son and her Lord.

2.   And we are *"blessed by ... Spirit"*. It is a unified relationship. Jesus offers us a holy, matrimonial and familial relationship with Him, a relationship of such UNITY.
If we wholeheartedly receive this incomparable gift of unified relationship, <u>through Jesus</u>, with the Father, Spirit and Mary, what could possibly ever frighten us again? What will we do with this powerful spiritual unity? How could it transform our lives? If we want it, it is an empowering gift to us for our <u>action </u>and application, in every area of our lives.

3.   *"Fear has no place in <u>My</u> world."* - God's will is clear. Fear is a trespasser, usurping the hearts and minds of many suffering people. It is being given its marching orders, because it has interfered with God's plans for faith, fruitfulness and joy, in what <u>is</u> His world.

4.   *"No words of wisdom can echo this.."* - refers to the best coping

strategies that the world's wisdom can offer to those suffering fear. No matter how helpful in calming the emotions, they will ultimately fall short if they accommodate fear or do not have the power to banish it completely. If the spiritual root remains, the plant will reappear, even in a modified form, and try again to choke or prevent faith.

5.   *"No longer will fear stalk the minds and hearts of My beloved. I am coming to set them free. Tell them ... so that I can anoint their ears with Truth, so lies gain no entry for fear....it is that easy...for I love them."*

Sometimes the sound of our thoughts can be so familiar that we fail to recognise the <u>voice of temptation and lies</u>, because it <u>seems</u> to come from within. Sown as tares among the wheat - and planted from many Godless and sometimes attractive sources, especially within multi-media, pragmatic cultural values, emotional connections, oppression, hurts, etcetera -   the lies that differ from the Word of God spring up and poison or strangle our souls through our mind and emotions. These lies gain entry into us, as enemy forerunners, for fear to root and grow in any of its many forms.
The Lord does not want this to continue and is offering a simple way of change. If we will only turn to Him and ask Him to (ff.6)

6.   *"anoint our ears with Truth"*, as He says, lies will no longer be able to gain entry for fear. If we soak in His Word, His Truth will set us free from fear and its manifold expressions; because we will have the anointed *discernment* which will allow us to ultimately recognise and reject the voice of lies. This will change our lives by freeing our hearts and minds to receive His wonderful healing love.

7.   *"No-one else loves like I do"* ff. - The rest of this piece is a passionate call to intimacy with the Lord. So much depends on our heartfelt desire for Him.

8.   *"Desire Me.. I might bless, with responses to hearts grown cold."* - By *desiring* Him, He will restore responses to frozen hearts.

2004

 I felt suddenly and unclearly stirred up, as though I was angry, but without any reason. It was different, in some hazy way, from my experience of being angry; and I decided not to investigate the 'feeling', (my habitual route to emotional information), but to ask God what was going on. His answer followed, <u>offering a life-changing strategy of going to Him **first**</u>, instead of to the place of deposited professional experience. He was moving my thinking, trained in limited analytical secular models, into His ways. He is the fount of all knowledge and wisdom, so why waste time and effort elsewhere?

"Who is knocking at my door?" 15 September

1.   *"The voice of anger, trying to get in"*. Although we feel anger, sometimes it can be external spiritual oppression, pressing in from the outside, (possibly even drawn to us by unacknowledged sin). But not everyone is alert to this in the emotional heat of the moment. To reduce the powerful emotional feeling of pressure, sometimes people talk about it in the belief that it will make things better. In the case of external oppression, talking about it with the person you are associating the anger with, can just make everything worse, because that actually opens the door and lets oppressive anger **in** to you.

   Then it turns up the heat and communication rapidly breaks down. It **intends** this. It is an enemy influence bent on destroying relationship, especially within families. Without discernment, mishandling anger can damage ourselves and others.

 Telling God instead opens the door to <u>Him</u> and oppression leaves, taking pressure with it.

Anger is no impediment to God and should never be allowed to keep us from Him. We do not need to suppress or repress the emotion, because He is a safe listener, whatever state we are in, and a gentle, peaceful receiver of everything that ails us. Shouting or crying to God does not alienate Him. Going to Him **first** means destructive, unrighteous anger can be banished, the emotions safely defused, truth and clarity restored; and reconciliatory communication with the other person(s) peacefully and constructively re-opened – at least from our side!

"Key to My Heart / Spend Time with Me/Truth..."
9 November
1. *"Truth is sustainable by faith, a choice underpinned."* - We choose Truth and underpin that choice by faith. So, our faith enables us to access, establish and maintain truth in our lives. Does this mean that by building our faith we increase our capacity for Truth and all it's power?
John 14 v.6: "I am the Way, the Truth and the Life."

When spiritual fear's strategic 'missiles' impact our lives, we experience them distractingly in our emotions; but faith is fear's real target, which explains why so many of God's people suffer from it. Sufficient emotional impact can blind us, drawing us away from prayerful Kingdom life and God's nourishing presence in scripture and holy Communion. This begins to starve or dry out any faith we have, thereby destabilising the position of Truth within us. People then 'feel' God has abandoned them, or is not real. Doubt enters, persuading fearful people to close down, or seek tangible refuge. 'Here and now' becomes the definition of 'real'. God no longer fits in the view of life, if He ever featured.

Neglecting to deal urgently with fear allows its corrosion to work. Its insidious influence can be nourished by 'entertainment' in films, books, T.V., computer games, music, etcetera. Accommodating any form that fools us into thinking it is harmless, breeds the familiarity that reduces its emotional impact. Fear intends this. People then become their own judges of what is acceptable, subjectively based on whether it 'hurts' or 'harms', or not. They assert their 'right to choose'.

Choices of this kind establish acceptability, the platform for fear, creating a stronghold for it to parasitically control people's lives and spread its influence to others. Temperaments change, behaviour alters, mental illness appears, confusion and violence is manifest – and Truth is successfully obscured from view, as increasing problems dominate vision. Immature believers weaken, not realising the imperative to guard their hearts. People get 'lost'. And all without conscious rejection of God and what He stands for. Faith, if anyone had any to start with, begins to look antiquated and redundant. So, in time, will God.

And so, fear captures and binds people's hearts, minds, lives.

But God has had enough and is intent on bringing about change. Mercifully, He offers to *"wash free with an anointing of Truth so great that many will fall on their faces in awe."*

If we will turn to Him, and spend time in His presence, He will restore Truth manifest in discernment, gentleness, peace and love
- to our core and to His world

2005

"My Blood is Thick Enough /We are Compassion"   **1 February**

1.   *"..days are hurtling towards the abyss - from where all hope comes."* - If life as we know it is hurtling towards its end, who will waste their remaining opportunities to turn to loving God?

'abyss' is defined as: bottomless gulf; the supposed water-filled cavity under the earth; primal chaos; hell; a measureless chasm; anything very deep (Chambers dictionary).

Even if we experience the abyss of loss, shock, trauma, pain,

261

wounds or anything else that sends us into free-fall sensation, God has still provided. In our personal abyss, **hope** is still there for us - if we want it. Without hope, the abyss is a place of bleakness.

2 *"Who...need(s)..hope when self proclaims all help?*
Materialist societies reward the achieving, empowered self. If all needs are viewed through this lens, material goals and personal striving can dominate the social landscape. Man's view of himself falsely inflates but, in reality, *shrinks* to his own capabilities and the material present. Self governs sufficiency. Society becomes intense, urgent and blind to its idolatry. Then, only the weak and the wise need hope.

3. *"In search of something of lasting worth, man seeks impact - a scurrilous counterfeit..* - People know there has to be more to life than self-satisfaction and many search for the unseen dimension. Spiritual counterfeits are everywhere. Even when seeking God, some believers primarily seek those spiritual experiences and sensations that accompany His manifest presence; because, for them, *'impact'* means 'God touched me', because sensation means real. Until He rebuked me, I did not realise how offensive this is to Him; or that I had been seeking Him thus 'safely', with a defended, closed heart.

4. *"...Path of Unknowing."*- is an insensate one, sometimes beyond understanding; a place of encounter, where we walk, or work, or wait, in God's presence for Him. Without sensory goals, we enter His mystery.

5. In the place of trust, we seek: the Lover for His sake; the Healer, not the healing; the Refiner, not the fire; the Comforter, not consolation; the Lord, not His minister. In deepest trust, we let Him choose *everything*.

6.   *"..baubles.."*- 'flashy' teachings demonstrate someone else's acquired knowledge of God. While these teachings and demonstrations can be useful in attracting attention to God, they are no substitute for an individual seeking Jesus for themselves.

7.   We cannot 'earn' our 'perfection' before God by our pain and suffering; and the incredible gift of salvation is not a reward or consolation prize for the sufferer. Our *'purified perfection'*, bestowed by the Spirit, is a blood bought, free gift through the suffering of Jesus <u>and</u> the Father.

8.   Together, they are Compassion, promising everything for us and ours, through the covering, purifying blood of Jesus.

"But I Fasted for You."   10 February
1.   Preparing especially for prayer one day, I bathed and used orange blossom lotion – a traditional bridal flower – that reminded me of missing the Bridegroom fast of the previous 3 days. I said: "I didn't fast for you, Lord.." and He replied *"But I fasted for you..."* and then continued.

2.   *"Show them the 'Way to My Heart'."*- see next word
     11 February ff.

3   a.*"..Dragon of.."* - i) often a guardian of treasure, ravaging a country when it's hoard is rifled.
ii) A fierce, intimidating or watchful person
     b.   *"..contempt..."* - scorn; disgrace; disregard for the rule of law; an offence against the dignity of ...
     c.   *"and false .."* - artificial or deceitful and dishonest form or expression of...
     d.   *"righteousness"* - wise, prudent, provoked or supported by a moral standpoint or premise; excellent, honest; straightness,

263

rightness, uprightness, integrity.

> False righteousness, therefore, is the antithesis of this definition. In this context it is any form of righteousness that is not rooted in God; and it can be present in some churches.

e. *"..dogs (My followers)."* - to track and watch constantly; to worry, plague, infest; to attach to stubbornly.

If the dragon's treasure is darkness and our believing presence is Christ's light in the world, we can expect to upset the dragon. So, the *"Dragon of contempt and false righteousness that dogs My followers"* means that followers of the Lord are being closely pursued by the contemptuous enemy, masquerading as righteousness.

One example is 'political correctness' that attempts to indoctrinate values through controls. Some of the values modify actual anti-social behaviour, justifying the application of the constraint; while others seek just to suppress or neutralise differences of opinion and beliefs. 'Incorrectness' can contravene legislation and lead to prosecution, so people learn to be cautious and self-conscious, or don public masks. In this way, fear in the form of unease is sown into the fabric of society.

I also understood that those the Enemy manages to deceive and infect could express this contemptuous and counterfeit face of evil, possibly inadvertently; and even within the church, and through impure teaching. This dragon's function is to corrupt, distort, deceive and ultimately ravage followers of the Lord; possibly by causing them to be contemptuous of truth in favour of 'masquerade', of something that only 'looks' good. For example, teaching can be corrupted by unscriptural opinion or 'popular' current understanding; worship can become distorted into socially relevant 'fun' performance, rendering it entertainment for a spectator congregation; charismatic leaders can draw attention to

264

themselves, stealing God's glory. When God is not the sole focus, an opportunity for holiness and intimacy can then lose to a 'good time in church'.

Every believer needs pure Truth and leaders carry a perilous level of responsibility.

4. Praise belongs <u>only</u> to God - it is sour to a disciple because it is <u>not</u> food for them.

"Way to My Heart" 11 February

1. *"..tyranny.."* - absolute or illegally* established power; the government or authority of a tyrant; oppression, cruelty, harshness. Fear is all these things.

"Unity / My Altar of Love" 8 March

1. *"..My little ones.."* - refers to paragraph 2 *"..the young, the old...the innocent."*

2. *"You give - they touch your heart."* - **NB** the order - we give first, <u>then</u> they touch our hearts, bringing us alive with Love. So modern day compassion fatigue could become nonsense. Giving to His *'little ones'* becomes a decision to do His will, not merely a response to an emergency or a catastrophe. We do not wait to be emotionally wrung by news or campaigns, because He has identified those *little ones* He wants us to help...**as a way of life.**

Unless we are called somewhere specifically, (and not including the extraordinary international crises that require our extraordinary responses), all we need to do is open our hearts to see those around us already. We are where we are for <u>each other's benefit</u>.

Because He is in all His *'little ones'*, it is Him we are helping. And we are brought to life through their response to our giving, which might not necessarily be comfortable or grateful, or personal. Giving brings life to the giver.

3.   *"..your lies.."* - refers to all false beliefs, including political, social, economic, emotional, psychological and spiritually false; (even those inadvertently established by man-made theology). Jesus <u>is</u> the Truth that exposes falseness.

4.   *"..I will dissipate the anger....transforming it into the POWER to love."* - Anger can be used for struggle and conflict - or, if given to God, transformed into the energy to love, equally fiercely. No-one needs to overcome in their own strength or let anger keep them from God. **He** will dissipate it; **He** will transform it. This is a message of hope for all victims (and perpetrators) of war, violence, assault, abuse, terror; and those governed by unpredictable temper.

"Love... poured out in Darkness"   16 May
1.   *"..before their light becomes too brilliant... to those who walk in darkness."*- see *'Fools for The Lord'* 2003. Those newly-saved from the darkness are best placed to immediately reach their still lost contemporaries. Ultimately, darkness shuns light.

2.   *"..in fullness of TRUTH."* - in Jesus, waiting in the place of anointing.

"I Am the Key (for the Unforgiven)"   16 June
This is a simple and immensely powerful promise of hope and healing, offered particularly to the <u>unforgiven</u> - those who know and can acknowledge that they have hurt others in some way and who may have been trying to make up for it, to repair the damage they did, or renew the relationships broken by their behaviour.
   There is no more despairing a place to be, no tighter chains around a penitent heart, no more stifling a place to have to live in than the place of withheld forgiveness.
   The gift of forgiveness can release burdens of shame and

sorrow. It brings light into darkness, particularly of memories. It soothes the scalding shame that sears beneath guilt.

To have sought forgiveness from another person, or hoped for it, and to be refused - or given hatred, violence, rejection, in return – can lead to hopelessness and unremitting guilt, or shut-down. It is hard, then, to be at peace; and people can get caught in a bind, trying to assuage guilt and perhaps trying to atone (possibly in a transferred way). This can produce its own shackles and treadmill.

So, this message is about freedom for the unforgiven - *if* they will only turn to the LORD. He promises to *"..release them from the yoke that binds them to the unforgiving others"*.

He will hear their honest and full account of their sin - for that is what it is - and He Himself will forgive them. By turning to Him, they will not only receive forgiveness, release, healing, new life, hope, a fresh start and all they need to live fully as God intended; but, by God's grace, they will guarantee the same for those they hurt, who themselves will then be set on a road to recovery from what was done to them.

(I don't know how, but I presume the unforgiving will experience an initial release or accelerated softening of their previous attitude, with or without their awareness. But God promises He will do it.)

2. *"If the sinner turns to Me, I will heal the sinned against."*

The repentant sinner who turns to the Lord for His forgiveness can secure the healing for their victim,
according to God's wonderful promise in this message.
The unforgiven can watch as God works this out - His invitation is equally clear. So to turn to God and confess sin brings blessing to everyone involved.

The unforgiven can be detached from their confessed sin. God's forgiveness of the sinner then breaks their connection (*'yoke'*) through sin to the hurt/ wounded/aggrieved withholders of forgiveness. Once released, they also can be freed to receive from God. He has promised to heal them, too. Take him at His word. It is <u>His</u> business. These are <u>His</u> ways. Who are we to argue?

3. *"..idols of satisfaction.."* are previously identified as *'pain', 'anguish', 'hatred', 'lies', 'scorn', 'enmity', 'cultural* divides'; and all that the words include in physical, mental and spiritual terms. *'Idols of satisfaction'* refer to that which can urgently demand our attention and energy to be relieved*, quietened, pacified, soothed, concealed, prioritised i.e. <u>to be satisfied</u>.

The driving need for satisfaction can bring those demands into position between us and God, so that they obscure our view and relationship with the Lord. That is idolatry. The beliefs, e.g. self-justification, which spring from trying to achieve these satisfactions can choke our hearts; and the idols bring dis-ease, malfunction, disorder, worry and chaos into our lives.

(*While recognising the very deep suffering that it can bring, sickness can also become idolatrous when it takes over and dominates the life of everyone involved, by eclipsing hope and life-giving faith and by dictating negative attitudes. While someone can become a vessel of sickness, the <u>person</u> is always more and bigger than the oppressive sickness, whatever the stage; and despite the temptation and opportunity to be overwhelmed by the pain and fear of the symptoms.)

4. *"I will vanquish the hordes...in lives that belong to Me."* -
The Lord is on the side of His people. HE will war against the enemies of those who turn to Him, especially the unseen demonic ones who play havoc in lives. He will deliver and rescue those who have placed their lives in His loving care.

"I Am the Depth, the Blessing, the Compassion."   9 July
1.   " *All for all.*" - He is All; we are all. Everything He is, He offers
to us.

2. " *..choices* made in establishment." - choices made and fixed, in
certain contexts, and not open to revision or change.
3.   *"Establishment"* - a place of fixed position, possession, or power;
proven, ordained, set up; the church established by law; the class
in a community or in a field of activity (e.g. government, church,
business company) who hold power, usually because they are
linked in some way (e.g. socially, similar status, etc.); and who are
considered to have conventional values or conservative opinions.
A permanent force; permanent staff; a person's residence,
household and style of living; a business; a settlement.
   Here, '*establishment*' means whatever we have built our lives on;
and /or given authority to, through <u>agreement</u>- even if the
agreement has been somehow forced on us by an abusive agent.
Agreements are the legal foundation for stronghold.

4. *"..castle of containment"* - a defensive tower, designed to prevent
(by means other than war) the spread of a power or influence
regarded as hostile.
In this context, our '*castles of containment*' are the defences we, as
individuals or organisations, build to self-protect against real or
imagined threat. They form mental strongholds. Churches are not
exempt. Disunity in the Body of Christ exemplifies the suspicion
that can exist between Christian denominations. Often our '*castles*'
are typified by rejection of someone or something different from us,
based on prejudice and often springing from fear. (NB **"Fools for
the Lord"** and **"Fear-Free World"**)
Despite feeling secure in such a castle, the Lord says that it really

5.   *"...is a castle of fear keeping in...brutalised beings"*, <u>locking in</u> our
compassion and <u>locking out</u> the needy and lost.

269

Fear itself is *"not an 'establishment"*, but *"a demolition"* - it is a ruining, or an action of pulling down. Fear is a destructive force. The message says that this defensive tower is a stronghold, but not of the Lord's making.

Because fear ruins, *"all that can reside in"* the defensive tower *"is that which contains, which limits, which curtails freedom"*. As builders of defences, we are 'king' of our 'castle'; but we are warned that inside our 'castles' we are really prisoners, ruled by the enemy. However, if we choose compassion, instead of self-preservation, our choice will free and bring us to God.

Even innocent victims and those whose fixed viewpoints ('establishment') includes experience of war can make a different choice. The Lord will enable them, if they so choose.

They can be freed, healed and released from their wounded anchorage, if they will only *"Cross the line."* In so doing, they will *"Defect from the Enemy"*, and be freed from fear. Then the Lord *"will make whole partial thinking, partitioned minds, brutalised beings."* He longs to heal because He is **"the depth, the blessing, the COMPASSION."**

6. *"..beautiful in their brutalising."* - No matter what has been done to us, or what damage we have inflicted on ourselves in any way, God claims us as HIS and calls us BEAUTIFUL. He sees us as He designed us to be and simply wants us to let Him heal us into that level of perfection which is His loving gift to us – and which we will not reach in our own independent strength.

7. *"..songs of righteousness.."* - some 'righteous' songs and sounds incite and disturb our spirits, begging the questions - Whose 'righteousness', opinion, or perspective, is being expressed? Whose voice and power is being exalted?"
In a literal sense, incitement can be especially true of secular music; and can be sensed in some church music which fails in performance to worship Him.

It also applies in a wider sense to media influences in general, which can generate disillusionment by resonating with negative experiences. This saps energy which God intends for joyful living, so He will bring an alternative 'song' for us to 'listen' to – the sound of contentment, carrying peace, which won't necessarily mean slow or quiet music, or even anything audible.

"Sacrifice"   15 August

NB the following quote (from *"I Am the Harvester"* 18 November 1991)

"Sacrifice is a hard word and is not self-denial. Sacrifice is self-giving. It is making of yourself an offering, as a lamb to the slaughter, as a bunch of grapes in the wine press, as an olive yielding oil. Without the gift there would be no produce. **Sacrifice is a gift, made in love, whatever the cost.**"

1.   *"The place of hardness....reckoning for all."* This is <u>not</u> suggesting that sacrifice should be announced, exhibited or paraded in an attention-seeking manner. But perhaps there should be no deliberate concealment. Part of the sacrificial gift is the cost to the giver - something that can be difficult, but sometimes important, for the <u>receiver </u>to handle. Often sacrificial givers conceal cost to avoid the beneficiary feeling uncomfortable, or sometimes to save themselves from feeling embarrassment; but, in saving their feelings, the giver deprives the receiver of the opportunity to develop appropriate appreciation - and the gift, apparently easily come by, can be undervalued or taken for granted.

   Sometimes sacrifice involves suffering messy, time-consuming change that cannot be confined to the comfort of privacy. What is truthfully there to be seen, sometimes has to be visible for everyone's benefit and growth - challenging givers and receivers. Just look at the cross.

3.   *"Your sacrifice was graceless"* - referred to an emotional melt-down the day before, when I scraped the memory barrel of any and every sacrificial thing I had ever done in my husband's direction. In many cases I had buried the cost, not paid it, as I had previously and piously believed. So I had gone through the motions of giving, but without actually letting go of the 'gift'. My idea of giving actually emotionally translated, for me, into loss. It all came out in one volcanic eruption when I had nothing left to give, but felt yet more was needed from me.

4.   *"..contained in their castles.."*
 see *" I Am the Depth..Compassion"* **9 July** footnote 3 ff. above.

5   *"..lying voice of temptation.."*   - When someone feels emotionally bankrupt, they can feel that the only thing left to them is to turn inward and hurt or destroy themselves. It is a timely, tempting, invasive, consuming **lie** - an enemy strategy - that presents a new and treacherous sense of power to the powerless. This **temptation** can be simply rejected and disempowered by stating the Truth - simply, although not necessarily easily.
    Underpinning true statements with declarations of scriptural Truth brings the Word of God against lies, changing the atmosphere and strengthening the speaker, who will experience the power of God at work. Speaking the Truth declares life. God gives us life in abundance, willing us to live it. What He wills, He enables us to do. We choose.
(This footnote in no way underestimates the place or intensity of suffering people can find themselves experiencing.)

6   *"..self-harmers.."* - all self-harmers e.g. addicts of any kind including drugs, alcohol, food, sex, pornography, horror, violence, or occult; people who cut or otherwise mutilate themselves; those with urges to self-destruct through suicide; or with blatant disregard for safety of themselves, or others, through reckless

self-daring.

(This is the most personally exposing piece in the whole book. It is included because it shows the Potter crumpling the misshapen pot and remoulding. The personal circumstances will not matter to the reader.

I share it to <u>show</u> to others the <u>infinite tenderness</u> they can <u>expect</u> at His hands at such a crucial time. If they are willing to allow it, God can add blessing for others' benefit.)

"More Lovers are Required/ The Armourer's Queue "
22 August

1.   *"All free offers as I break My body and feed you in loving sacrifice."* - This refers to Jesus giving His life for each one of us and feeding us with Himself, in a <u>continuous</u> way - and drawing attention to the significance of the holy Eucharist as a unique source of direct nourishment from Jesus, freely and personally given, every time.

2.   *"Do not take lightly the gifts of My Church."* – A command to know and respect the gifts, including sacraments; and not to overlook them in the pursuit of changing topical forms.

3.   *"Do not relinquish the time-honoured truths for spur-of-the-moment novelty. No one can recreate the finest, which I breathed life into."* - In the days of hunger and thirst for God, it is so easy to search for the new and impacting; and overlook the **fact** that we have already been provided for in the finest way, by Jesus Himself, as He breaks his body and feeds us with it - as shown in Luke 22 v.19-20:
'And he took bread, gave thanks and broke it, and gave it to them, saying, *"This is my body given for you; do this in remembrance of me."*
There is no substitute.
Also, the believers in the <u>earliest</u> church "..devoted themselves to the apostles' teaching and to fellowship, *to the breaking of bread* and to prayer." Acts 2 v.42

"Lovers Call Warriors"   23 November

1.   *"..trees rooted in haste, in shallow ground."* - refers to the proliferation of church <u>leaders</u>, especially those not rooted in love, or properly mature.

"You Are What You Eat...I Cannot Be Displaced - I AM" Christmas Eve 2005

1. *"..prisoners of their own making are forced to come out.* - Fearful self-protection will prove to be inadequate. There will be deliverance from strongholds of fear.
*(**N.B**. "I Am the Depth, the Blessing, the Compassion" July 2005; footnote 3 - 'castle of containment')*

2.   *"Pandemonium..."* - in Milton's poem 'Paradise Lost', this is the capital of Hell. It is a very disorderly, noisy place or assembly; tumultuous uproar.

3.   *"..but a Word will bring calm. A single Word will be spoken to render harm harmless."* - Jesus is the Word.

4. *"..to make Me fit the places of position.."* Whenever I had a sense of what Jesus asked of me, I tried to take up that place and see Him from that position - a new vantage point meant a new image or perspective. He showed me that in trying to consider Him in relational ways, e.g. as <u>my</u> friend, <u>my</u> brother, <u>my</u> lover, <u>my</u> consoler, I had been trying to see Him in those roles: thereby trying to *'fit'* Him into those *'places of position'*, somehow making Him in 'my' image. No wonder I couldn't see Him clearly...

But, all the time, <u>He</u> has been moulding me to become <u>His</u> friend, <u>His</u> lover, **<u>His!</u>** The emphasis here is that if Jesus is e.g. our friend, our lover, that makes each of us <u>His</u> <u>chosen</u> friend, His <u>chosen</u> lover. How does that realisation affect our view of ourselves?

274

5. *"You chose LIFE."* - Deuteronomy 30 v.19-20: **'This day I set before you life and death, blessings and curses. Now choose life, so that you and your children may live and that you may love the Lord your God. Listen to His voice and hold fast to Him. For the Lord is your life..'**

In 1991, after being diagnosed with M.E., a friend introduced me to Derek Prince's teaching on 'Blessings and Curses'. I chose to believe the above scripture and subsequently God completely healed me from M.E. I continued to use 'life' as a guide in other areas.

6. *"You are not to worry..."* - All concerns then fell from me, except for 'Diary of the Lord'. Another miracle!

7. *"Just as I would have died only for you...you must live as though.. salvation."*- Just as Jesus would have gone to the cross if only one person lived on earth, so each individual must fulfill God's full calling - we must <u>each</u> live as if we were the only living example of a follower of Jesus. Our commitment and integrity must be total and without compromise. We choose, He enables us.

8. *"It is My birthday. It is yours."* - refers to Christmas Day 1979 when I woke up after a Christmas Eve encounter with a stranger who knocked on my door... Jesus came to me, moved into me and changed my life forever. I had no idea what was happening and had never heard of such a thing. He was there for about four hours - long enough for me to fall in love with Him - before He told me who He was.....

9. *" - because I Am greater than all."* - Jesus is LORD. Mary is His gift. Receiving His gifts cannot displace Him. But no received gift must be given the <u>primary focus due to the Giver,</u> or idolatry can creep in. This is true for all gifts - such as worship styles, ministry gifts, revival, anointed speakers, saints, signs and wonders,

etcetera.

Attend to the Giver, who alone selects and distributes His gifts appropriately.

10. **NB** We **must** get the Word of God **inside** us.

"Take Courage To The Nations" 30 December

1.   *"Take courage, from the place of fearlessness."* The place of fearlessness is a source of Courage and Delight; and the previous piece above (*"You Are What You Eat"* invites us to walk in this place and enjoy it. This message encourages us to draw on those resources and *"Take courage to the nations."* as a powerful, liberating gift from the Lord.

2.   *"Soak and be washed clean of the traces of burdens."* - See *'Love - The River/ Ocean of Timeless Love'* July 1986.

3.   *"..repeat the LIVING that My tired and aching world requires."* - the LIFE model is given above.

2006

"Today's Bread / Come to the Feast of Tabernacles" 24 February

1. *"What if I change My mind?"* - This is **not** a contradiction to Numbers 23 v.27, which speaks of God's constancy and single-mindedness:

"God is not a man, that he should lie; or a son of man, that he should change His mind."

While the Lord Himself is constant, He can change his response or position towards something as He chooses - because He is God. This is a warning against presumption and the corruption of the over-familiar approach to God that can deceive people into falsely feeling they can know Him - in the sense of getting the measure of

Him, which can lead to spiritual arrogance or taking God for granted. While we can always trust Him, He also commands our awe.

It is an <u>encouragement to stay in reverent, constant, closest communion with Him; and to follow His leading Spirit.</u>

2.   *"I Am fresh, new every morning. Today's bread is for today - not tomorrow; and it cannot feed yesterday. And it cannot be...saved for another day."* - as Jesus taught His disciples to pray in the Lord's Prayer : "Give us, this day, our <u>daily</u> bread..".

3.   *"..the Bread of Life"* - is Jesus Himself, Word made flesh.

4.   *"How much fresher can it be than Body to body?"* He Himself wants to feed us directly, (His) Body to (our) body, with nothing and no one in between.

This is also another reference to holy Eucharist as His physical source of daily Bread of Life; and is a reminder to churches which have neglected the model of the Fellowship of the Believers in Acts2 v.42 - teaching, fellowship, breaking of bread and prayer.

All four elements were present in the first Church, where (Acts 2 v.43) *"Everyone was filled with awe, and many wonders and miraculous signs were done by the apostles."*

5. *"Can't you hear Me calling you, to come to the **Feast of Tabernacles**?"*

The Feast of Tabernacles (Sukkoth) was instituted by God through Moses, consisting of a week's presentation of burnt offerings, but beginning and ending with a sacred assembly. It coincided with the dedication of the Temple, the permanent resting place for the Ark of the Covenant which held God's laws.

The Feast of Tabernacles <u>celebrates God's protection</u> of Israel, and His <u>provision</u> for their needs, <u>as they wandered in the desert</u>

277

for forty years before entering the promised land.

The purpose and importance of this Feast was for Israel to reflect and renew their commitment to God and trust in His guidance and protection.

Taking this as a model: could beginning and ending the weeks of our lives with a sacred assembly and daily feeding on the Word in both forms cause us to be able to live the Feast of Tabernacles, expecting His protection and provision as a normal way of life, independent of the world's systems?

Interestingly, a sacred assembly on the first and last days of the week would combine the nominated Sabbaths of Jews and Christians.

6. *"..your tabernacle."* - the human body is regarded as the temporary abode of the soul and is sometimes, therefore, called a tabernacle; but God nourishes our whole being, so tabernacle here must also mean everything that we are. He wants to nourish all that we are.

7. *"My Tabernacle.."* is the very heart of God Himself.

It is also the place of **exchange**, where our daily life can be renewed and our daily 'deaths' (e.g. hurts, concerns, sacrifices) consumed. If we will release all of ourselves, daily, into Him, we will be constantly purified, renewed and ultimately transformed into lovers and light bearers for His sake and for the sake of our world. The Feast of Tabernacles and feeding daily on new bread are a metaphor for life on earth.

   In our daily life, we need to remember we are temporarily on the earth, and this invitation is to accept our loving Lord's provision of His essential nourishment and protection as we too journey through life, through deserts and purification processes, into His Tabernacle, His Heart - our permanent home.

   These amazing words of **fulfilment** and **completion** bring together the old and new feasts of salvation - Tabernacles and Bread – saying that the combination is essential:

"Only those who enter the Tabernacle of My heart can feed on new bread."

This is also a clear signpost to the future of faith – somehow the **people** of the Old Covenant and the **people** of the New Covenant **must** unite and consume the same Bread:

"Nourish, or die – the choice is yours."

AMEN.

Please consider sharing these precious messages with someone else who might benefit.

If you give your copy away and would like a replacement, please contact the publishers and they will help.

Otherwise, copies may be purchased through retail outlets and on-line, or direct from BethBara Books (details p.4).

If you would like to share your responses to the *'DIARY'* or want any more information, please contact the writer through BethBara Books or at

www.diaryofthelord.com

Writer's Biography.

Viv Walsh was born in 1951 in South Wales and spent her professional life in Hampshire, working in education and the NHS. She is married to a 'saint' (who, naturally, objects to the title) and is the mother of two truly 'amazing, humbling' sons. All three men in her life are 'alpha' males, so she's trained in survival. She is grateful for the graceful influence of her beautiful daughter-in-law; and that in 2009 God has planned for her to become a granny - so she's looking forward to 'wearing purple' and kissing tiny cheeks.

To Margaret and John,
A gift of love,
Viv.